BUSI

WARFARE

Management for Market Conquest

Quek Swee Lip

BUSINESS WARFARE

Management for Market Conquest

Pelanduk
Publications

Published by
Pelanduk Publications (M) Sdn. Bhd.,
24 Jalan 20/16A, 46300 Petaling Jaya,
Selangor Darul Ehsan,
Malaysia.

All correspondence to:
Pelanduk Publications (M) Sdn. Bhd.,
P.O. Box 8265, 46785 Kelana Jaya,
Selangor Darul Ehsan, Malaysia.

Perpustakaan Negara Malaysia   Cataloguing-in-Publication Data

Quek, Swee Lip
    Business Warfare: management for market conquest/
    Swee Lip Quek; illustrations by Allan Miller.
    ISBN 967-978-564-5
    1. Business. 2. Business planning. 3. Marketing.
    I. Miller, Alan. II. Title.
    658

Printed by
Eagle Trading Sdn. Bhd.

CONTENTS

FOREWORD

The relationship between military thinking and strategy and management thinking and strategy is increasingly recognised as close. In Britain, until recent years, the vast majority of senior managers had experience of military service through conscription. Many managers still gain that experience through voluntary service in the Officers Training Corps or the Territorial Army and through short commissions in the armed forces. Those that have had this dual experience recognise the parallels and the transferability of lessons from the one situation to the other.

For many managers the military experience is not one that they will have at first hand. In the West, where military service is increasingly confined to limited numbers, generally of men, the majority of business people will have to learn about military ideas second hand through books.

In recent years there has been an upsurge in military thinking in relation to business thinking. Many of the classics of military strategy such as Carl von Clausewitz's *On War* are to be found on the reading lists for strategy courses. The United States Marine Corps manual *Warfighting* has recently been published as a management text prefaced by the reflections of a number of senior executives on their own days in the marines and what these meant for their later approach to business.

In part this interest in the West may stem from an increased awareness of the role of military thinking in the business philosophy of the East. The Japanese, for example, use the analogy of soldiers to describe the role and objectives of managers. The concept of economic warfare does not carry the negative overtones in the East that it does in the West.

Swee Lip Quek in his book *Business Warfare* has taken as his starting point one of the great military thinkers of the East, Sun Tzu, and demonstrated how the ideas of a soldier can be developed through the management ideas with which we are familiar to achieve even greater business success. Starting with the importance of vision and strategy he then leads the reader through issues of internal management and marketing for the modern corporation.

Business Warfare is an accessible book for any manager but at the same time is full of challenge. Each chapter gives the reader short extracts both in written and pictorial form from Sun Tzu's masterpiece and whets the appetite for more of his insights. These pointers to key aspects of strategy and implementation are then worked through in the more familiar language and concepts of contemporary management debate. Each chapter gives the reader a framework for thinking about a particular aspect of management as well as practical advice, examples and clear conclusions.

Parts of the culture and outlook of the soldier can be transferred to the manager in his or her organisational setting. Swee Lip Quek portrays the need for commitment and urgency on the part of the soldier business person. Without this stance, the manager cannot set a path and lead. Throughout the book, Dr Quek urges the manager to clarity, alertness and conviction in his or her assessment of situations, planning and action. He warns in a very chilling phrase of the dangers of doing anything less when he states that 'survival is not compulsory'.

Business Warfare is a book which will be enjoyed by practising managers and anyone who is interested in how business and organisations can survive in an increasingly competitive marketplace. By taking examples and analogies from a different world, that of the soldier, Quek challenges the reader to think about what being a businessperson and a manager is ultimately about. He also gives the reader a rich array of pointers and techniques built upon classic management thinking which can help the soldier business person achieve his or her goals more readily.

Dr Carol Vielba
Director, Evening MBA, City University Business School

My thanks ....

To Pop, for teaching me to focus on the important, rather than the urgent.

To Mom, for being living proof that perserverence is the mother of success.

To my wife, Fui Mee, for teaching me the strength in gentleness and the wisdom in patience.

To my daughters, Lee Huang and Lee Ann, for giving me the precious moments I draw on for comfort and inspiration.

To the others whose love and friendship I am blessed with, for showing me that loyalty is the rock on which all other virtues are founded.

It is my privilege to dedicate this book to all of you.

TRUE EXCELLENCE IS TO SUBDUE THE ENEMY WITHOUT FIGHTING...

INTRODUCTION

Once upon a time in ancient China, there lived four great warriors. They were the closest of friends, and had taken a solemn oath of eternal brotherhood.

One fine autumn day, the four of them happened to be sharing a meal at their favourite inn. The food was good, and the wine plentiful. They were in fine spirits. Before long they were regaling each other with their combat experiences.

As their trust for one another was absolute, they began to share the secrets of their success.

The largest of the four was the first to disclose his winning technique. 'There is no one stronger than I. The way I despatch my opponent is fast, effective and conclusive. I pounce on him, grab him in a bear hug and squeeze the life out of him. If that doesn't work, my powerful punches and kicks will always finish the job.'

The next man then spoke up. 'I do not believe in force against force. My method is to borrow the strength of my enemy and then use it against himself. I wait for my enemy to attack. When he does, I offer no resistance, but instead *receive* his force. Pulling him towards me, I will then throw him to the ground with deadly force. Finishing him off after that is usually a straightforward matter.'

The third man, who by now had a look of amusement on his face, then took his turn to speak. 'You are both magnificent warriors'. Turning to the first speaker, he said, 'You, my brother, are huge and strong. Since I am of slighter build, and not quite as strong as you, your methods will not work for me.' Turning to the second speaker, he continued, 'You use skill as opposed to brute force. That I like better. But, you are still taking unnecessary risk, as you place yourself within striking reach of your opponent. Your technique still necessitates physical contact. Accidents and miscalculations can happen. Your method is too dangerous for me.'

Pausing to finish his tea, he then explained his approach. 'What I do is effective and safe. I observe my enemy for days, or even longer. I watch his goings in and out, and learn his movements, behaviour and habits. Using my knowledge, I set a trap into which my enemies invariably fall. Thus, I not only fight from a safe distance, I am the invisible enemy.'

The last speaker, a diminutive man with a prominent forehead, had been silent till now. He had meditated attentively over all that had been said. When he was invited to speak, he did so with deliberate slowness.

'Victory and safety are vital considerations. Sustained victories can only come with the application of wisdom. Brute force alone is seldom enough, and can be dangerous to oneself, as you have said (acknowledging the former speaker with a respectful nod). *True excellence is to subdue the enemy without fighting . . . and to do so in such a way that one does not expose oneself to either immediate danger or to future retribution.*'

Continuing, he (who did not look much of a warrior) elaborated, 'The result of my technique is that nobody even notices me. As far as everybody is concerned, I am uninvolved. True invisibility is when your enemies do not notice that you are the enemy. My technique involves either getting my enemy to entrap himself or *to use a borrowed knife.'*

The term *to use a borrowed knife* means to get some other, usually unwitting, party to do the killing.

All business is about war. Whether evident or not, businesses are constantly engaged in warfare. In managing war, the ultimate aim should be to *win without fighting.* This principle is stated clearly in that great thesis on strategic warfare, *The Art of War* written by Sun Tzu some 2,500 years ago.

One reason for the need to be unnoticed, and to be unimplicated, is that the vanquished will often seek revenge, and thus victory for the victor may be tenuous.

This principle parallels the business ideal:

Maximum gain with minimum cost, and at minimum risk.

Rather than seek to harm the opposition, the wise man will aim to turn the enemy into a friend. Acquiring a genuine ally is a far superior option to *losing* an enemy. Success in this quest will result not only in the permanent elimination of the threat, but the acquisition of the strength of a friend.

The consistent use of a Win-Win approach is the best way of securing genuine and mutually beneficial commitments. By such means we may secure valuable allies. As the wise know all too well, there is strength in gentleness.

One should never forget that the ultimate purpose of war is peace. As General Douglas McArthur stated, true soldiers are not warmongers. They, more than anyone else, desire peace – for soldiers pay most dearly in times of war.

Many underperform and fail in business and life, because they fail to discipline themselves in thinking, planning and behaving like soldiers at war.

In times of peace, prepare for war, and in times of war, prepare for peace.

The most crucial task in the preparation for war is building a disciplined and expert team. Without this no battle plan, no matter how well laid out, will prosper. Thus, nurturing respect, loyalty, unity, and obedience is a crucial responsibility of the general, and of chief executives and managers. Constant training and preparation are critical success factors that cannot be exaggerated: in war, in business, and in life.

Those who shudder at the thought of applying martial concepts and analogies in business must be realistic. The world is full of people who see themselves as 'martyrs', while the rest of the world sees them only as failures. Wisdom, discipline, and aggression are virtues which need to be cultivated at all costs.

It is widely recognised that the Japanese base their business strategies on the principles of war. This explains why books such as *The Art of War*; *The Romance of the Three Kingdoms*; *The Water Margin*; and *The Book of Five Rings*, are so widely read among CEOs of Japanese multinationals.

Business failure all over the world is occurring at an increasingly alarming rate. The future for many organisations, both new and established, looks little brighter.

Many reasons for this phenomenon have been offered. These include international political upheavals, rising interest rates, inflation, exchange rate volatility, overseas competition, credit squeeze, and worsening industrial relations. Yet many of these glibly offered excuses are mere *stonewalls*.

I should like to offer my definition for stonewalling: a refusal to accept the truth or acknowledge errors; constant attribution of failure to factors and circumstances 'beyond our control'. In so doing, the opportunity to learn and benefit from mistakes is lost.

The truth of the matter is, in many cases, painfully simple and straightforward. The core cause and principal culprit is *mismanagement*.

Mismanagement is the failure of management to manage effectually.

Where the 'generals' are unable to assess the implications of developing circumstances and future scenarios, how can they position their 'armies' to exploit the choicest opportunities, while avoiding the dangers and pitfalls (which await the unwary)?

Knowledge and the ability to act decisively and effectively (based on that knowledge) will always be the hallmarks of the real champions and great generals.

The scene is set for lean, hungry, fast, flexible and innovative companies led by strategically-minded chieftains to steal away the market share from lumbering 'giants' – giants who, once mighty and prosperous, have of late grown fat and sluggish, and increasingly unable to defend their territories.

Change is now truly global. Never has this statement been more true than it is today. Who would have hought just five or six years ago that the likes of China, Thailand and even Vietnam could change so dramatically? Never has change been so rapid and complex – and it will only become more so as we race toward the next century.

The key to making sense out of confusion is to go to the

roots of change. Once the cause is known, the symptoms will come to make sense and become easier to predict and prepare for. *Confusion which grips the enemy* is a potent weapon indeed to those strategists who can perceive their secrets with crystalline clarity.

The nature of competition is changing, becoming more global, and growing in wisdom and sophistication. The stakes are now much higher than before. In halcyon days, competition was local, national, or regional. Now, the prize is the world.

In any marketplace, protectionism is being attacked, and although there are many who would still resist free competition, they cannot hold back the tide of global change for long. Consequently, businesses and nations that are to survive must awake to reality. Unless they begin to train, think and behave with the opportunistic aggression of predators and warriors, they stand to lose everything.

As for customers, with every passing day, they have access to far more information, and have greater choice from the increasing array of products, services and suppliers. The unmistakable trend: **price *per se* no longer determines choice and re-purchase behaviour: Comparative Value Imaging does!**

Consider also the methods and techniques used to run yesterday's businesses. These will not work for the businesses of tomorrow. Business and management are changing by revolution rather than by evolution.

'Engineering and exploiting change' must be the operative commandment. It is no longer sufficient to be a beneficiary of change, for the advantage is shared with competitors and the time to reap the benefits is short. The goal must be to bring about change and be in a position to exploit that change fully. Thus, the strategic aim should be to **astonish**:

to the delight of the customer, and to the confusion of our competitors. **As in war, the ultimate aim is to stand alone in peace in the battlefield of our choice**.

The alternative to winning is failure. To paraphrase Dr Edwards Deming, the pioneer of Total Quality Control in early post-War Japan:

You don't have to do this. After all, survival is not compulsory.

THE AUTHOR

Dr Quek Swee Lip is the founder and Chief Executive of the SynerGem Group, a leading strategic consultancy specialising in Eastern Europe. Since the fall of communism in the former Comecon bloc, he has consulted across a wide spectrum of sectors and has advised Czechoslovak and Czech ministers on industrial, economic and foreign trade strategies. Dr Quek is currently assisting major manufacturers to develop markets in Asia and the United Kingdom.

With a Bachelor's degree in Business Administration from the University of Singapore, Dr Quek went on to gain an MSc (with distinction) from the London School of Economics and an MBA from the City University Business School. He subsequently received a doctorate for his thesis on strategic management. He has also received his higher doctorate (Doctor of Science) from the Technical University of Ostrava for his thesis and work on the practical application of military strategy to global business and economies. In addition, he is an associate of the Institute of Taxation and a fellow of both the Chartered Institute of Management Accountants and the Chartered Association of Certified Accountants.

1

VISION – MISSION – CULTURE

Without vision, the people perish.

Proverbs 29: 18.

'Strategy begins with a vision'.

Alfred Herrhausen,
the late CEO of Deutschebank.

The vision, to any organisation, is like a guiding star to the nomads and seafarers of old.

To be without a clear and true vision, is to not know where we should be heading for. To not know our destination, is to be ignorant of the direction we should be taking.

To not know the right direction, is to head for trouble and danger – and this can often be fatal!

The tragedy is that though many businesses are lost and are wandering aimlessly, few realise it – and even fewer do anything to remedy this core problem.

Begin with Vision

Let us be clear why we are placing so much emphasis on **vision**. Organisations and individuals who win and keep on winning are usually powered by more than mere inborn talent or luck; they have something which the rest lack: vision.

A vision is an ultimate goal. It usually begins life as a fantasy. But, with time and nourishment, the fantasy turns into something which gives energy.

A true vision is an awe-inspiring and attitude-changing picture of what we aspire to for our organisation (or ourselves). It is something which causes an individual or a team to persist in a given direction despite their own inadequacies and regardless of the obstacles. An effective vision will inflame an entire organisation with a deep and penetrating sense of unity and purpose. In lean times, a searing vision will empower the members of the organisation, individually and as a team, to grow strong and wise from the trials.

A true vision is thus like a cleansing fire. It will burn away the impurities of short-termism and impulsiveness.

Unity is a critical success factor in the fulfilment of a vision. There are, however, numerous instances in the history of mankind, where betrayal and resistance have worked positively to strengthen resolve and commitment – and to make the realisation of the vision even more urgent. Yet, at the end of the day, unity of at least a core group is necessary for any vision to be changed into reality. A united and motivated team, though small, is much more than a match for an uncoordinated rabble, and unity is born of a common vision.

Without harmony in the state, no military expedition can

2

A UNITED AND MOTIVATED TEAM, THOUGH SMALL, IS MUCH MORE THAN A MATCH FOR AN UNCOORDINATED RABBLE, AND UNITY IS BORN OF A COMMON VISION.

3

be undertaken; without harmony in the army, no battle array can be formed.

Sun Tzu.

To be of real and substantial value to any organisation, the vision adopted should be most, if not all, of the following:

- challenging and inspiring – but achievable;
- focused on meeting the needs of the customer;
- easily and naturally understood, remembered and identified with by everyone in the organisation: the rule here is that the vision statement should be short and simple – but dynamite!;
- broad enough so as not to obstruct innovation within the core business;
- actually shared by everyone in the organisation, and be evident in their culture and behaviour: i.e. it should form the foundation of the organisation's culture and philosophy;
- a guiding star to sustain ongoing effort to maintain the 'ultimate state' once it has been attained.

As an example, Synergem's vision is to become:

the most trusted partners in the world.

Great visions inspire, refresh, unite, and provide tremendous sense of purpose.

They sustain organisations through difficult times. And there will always be difficult times.

However, great visions do not become real in the minds and hearts of people overnight. Things take time – and great things often take lots of time. But this process of core-transformation often takes too much time because top managers are too often oblivious to the fact that one of their most critical key roles is to spread their vision to every

4

single member of the organisation. Patience is essential: lack of resolve is a principal reason for failure. Potentially wonderful visions are abandoned after a few confrontations with problems and disappointments. These, though extremely disillusioning at times, are inevitable realities. Champions see them for what they truly are: trials sent to refine and strengthen.

A diamond, in its natural state, is unlovely to look at. Yet the potential beauty and worth that lies beneath the outer skin of that rock makes all the planning, skill, time, effort and care needed to cut and polish it into its final state completely worthwhile. So it is with a true vision. Often we think we see the full vision. Yet invariably, with the passage of time, and as we progress in experience, skill, and wisdom, we will be thrilled by fresh discoveries of new facets of that gem that we had never been able to see before.

By going to the very core problem in our analysis of numerous corporate failures, we find recurringly that the core problem lies in the absence of a unifying corporate vision. We are not surprised by our findings, for the history of great men, women, and movements is full of monuments to this truth.

Those who scoff at the importance of a vision are shallow in their understanding, and will be victims of their own arrogance and ignorance. The importance of having a vision may not be apparent in good times, but when the storms strike, and there is no rock (vision) to hold on to – and to rally the 'troops' – great will be the fall and destruction. At best, the 'vision-less' will survive, but only just. And even then, they will be seen and be scorned as mediocre 'also-rans'.

From Vision to Mission

As we have already seen, a vision which sets hearts alight with passion, and is so true that the passion may be sustained, will give rise to a deep-seated sense of mission. The vision must create and fuel a spirit of enterprise.

This mission will (and must) become the very reason for an organisation's existence. It should thus be carefully and unrelentingly nurtured to become the underlying motive and guide for all plans and actions. All our activities, efforts, and plans must be focused on the successful achievement of the mission. The mission therefore, focuses action, optimises the application of resources, and eliminates wastage.

Having been developed from the vision, the mission statement (which puts in words what the mission is) must necessarily define how we are to achieve our vision. Put another way, a mission statement answers the question: what business are we in?

For the statement to achieve the resultant organisational change and unity of purpose, it is vital that it be shared by every single member of the organisation. The leaders, especially the chief executive, are the principal custodians of this *legacy*.

For the legacy to be effectively *inherited*, the statement must be worded so that it contains just one simple core thought.

A great vision should be based on the vision of the target customers. Therefore, the resultant mission statement must be something which can supercharge not only the members of the organisation, but even their customers and other allies. A mission statement of this kind can be used very effectively for marketing, and in particular, public relations purposes. It must be one which can lodge firmly in the minds of the target audience and then be nurtured to bear rich fruit.

Unless the vision is a true vision which is effectively shared by all members of an organisation, and unless there is a

6

strong sense of purpose, the mission statement is unlikely to be of any practical worth.

To illustrate again using our own experience, in developing Synergem's vision, our resultant mission statement became:

> *Blessing customers, our people, and allies with the strengths that we are gaining.*

Giving Substance to the Mission

We operate today under conditions of increasing turbulence and growing competitive aggressiveness. For organisations to be motivated, innovative, fast, and flexible, they can no longer afford to be structured like corporate dinosaurs, i.e. vertical, hierarchical, and bureaucratic.

Bureaucratic organisations do one thing very well: they stifle creativity and innovation. Such entities, when stripped of external protection (politically inspired or otherwise), will not survive in today's business environment.

The mission must thus be clear, but not rigid. Flexibility to act in order to exploit change must be maintained. On the issue of flexibility, listen to the words of the great strategist:

> *Water shapes its course according to the nature of the ground over which it flows; the soldier works out his victory in relation to the foe whom he is facing. . . . He who can modify his tactics in relation to his opponent, and thereby succeed in winning, may be called a heaven-born captain.*
>
> Sun Tzu.

The organisations that will survive and prosper tomorrow must motivate rather than obstruct. They must be orientated towards empowering rather than stultifying: to say 'yes' rather than 'no'. Flat organisations (those with minimal levels of control) will thrive. Well organised, multilevel marketing organisations are living proof of this.

Prosperous organisations will increasingly be characterised and distinguished from others by their highly motivated, autonomous, and expertly trained teams. Where the practice will enhance performance, teams will be transformed into investment centres, vested with the responsibility, authority and accountability to make sales (even though these sales might be to other teams within the organisation), profits, and investments.

These investment centres (or at least 'profit' centres – i.e. like investment centres, but without the authority to make capital investments) should be encouraged to develop their own mission statements. These 'lower level' mission statements will be derived from (and will therefore contribute to) the achievement of the organisation's overall mission statement).

A machining department might have as its mission statement:

> To contribute to overall productivity by getting things right first time, every time.

For a few moments, (preferably with one or more colleagues) consider the in-depth, practical and motivational implications of the above mission statement.

Culture Statement

The culture statement is a potentially very powerful aid to Total Quality Management (which we will look at in Chapter 4). Sadly, however, it is developed by few organisations and actually used by even fewer. Yet, if this is participatively developed, and effectively shared by every member in the organisation, it can help improve and sustain effectiveness and efficiency throughout the organisation in numerous powerful ways.

The culture statement complements the mission statement by elaborating the philosophy and principles which will govern, not only our strategies, but everything we do. The statement takes the form of a list of words or phrases which should be used as a guide – and as criteria – for developing and selecting strategies, policies and operating practices.

For example, a culture statement may include the following:

- always find out exactly what the customer wants;
- delight the customer without fail;
- never be guilty of bureaucracy;
- our word is our bond!

Even though keeping things short and simple is important for effectiveness, each 'headline' term should be clearly developed into operating statements or policies which can be used to practically define and control the way things are done.

Concrete definitions of elements in the culture policy should be developed to include clear standards. These then become the basis for a **control system** which will help to bring about organisation-wide uniformity of excellence in all key areas.

Making Systems Work

No matter how well designed, there will always be the odd design fault that needs to be rectified. Consequently, no operational system or policy should be seen to be carved in stone. There is always room for improvement.

Flexibility is vital. New knowledge and conditions must be reflected in the way we do things to ensure that improvement is never-ending and that competitive edge is maintained.

Although time consuming, especially at the outset, an effective monitoring system must be in place to measure results of performance and to match these against targets. Variances, both negative and positive (it is so tempting to manage only by negative exception), must be causally analysed. Findings must consistently, clearly and in timely fashion, be communicated to relevant parties. Action is, however, the key; not the information. Information generated by any such system is useless unless acted upon – either to change behaviour or method, or to change the way standards and targets are set. Consequently the product of such a system must be action-oriented information.

Many systems do not work or are not maintainable because top level commitment is missing. Management cannot expect junior personnel to practise what they are not seen to be seriously practising themselves. There is no factor more important to the successful implementation of a system than top level commitment. Other critical success factors are participative design involving all key parties and effective systems of feedback (appraisal, rewards, and reprimands) based on performance.

Buzz-words

Words must have meaning. Vision, mission and culture statements and the policies derived from them must motivate action. Too often, however, policies are churned out in spaghetti fashion and become pure gobbledegook, wholly confusing to those who are meant to carry out the policies.

Elaborated below are four buzz-words which are often used all too glibly without understanding what is actually required in practical terms:

Swift: to be swift requires getting rid of flab (primarily bureaucracy which satisfies administrators rather than customers) and resistance to change; and bringing about turbocharging teamwork that will eliminate weak links (and thus bottlenecks) and enable smooth and speedy operations from start to finish.

Swift does not mean hasty. Haste truly makes waste. Moving effectively and swiftly can only happen if obstacles are identified in advance and avoided. This cannot happen if one is moving in ignorance or blind haste.

Flexible: no organisation can be flexible unless its people are flexible. Flexibility can only be truly part of the corporate culture if top managers are flexible in their thinking. As with success and achievement, flexibility begins in the mind. Flexibility means, *inter alia*, never concluding an argument by stonewalling:

> *We've always done it this way, so we're not about to change now!*

The saying 'if it isn't broken, don't mend it' is no longer good enough. If we are truly seeking to be the best, we must always be on the lookout for new opportunities. And new opportunities often necessitate changes. Just because a practice, policy or work method is not fundamentally defective, it does not mean that it should not be changed. Total Quality is based not only on quantum leaps brought about by technology, but also by the small, 'creeping' improvements that are often the result of applied common sense. These small changes should not be despised, for their implementation not only results in technical improvements but also in improved morale: people need to feel that they are treated seriously.

Our operative motto *must* thus be: *if it isn't best – it isn't good enough!*

Proactive: probably one of the most used terms, but also the most superficially understood.

11

To be proactive means to read the early warning signs and plan and act accordingly to pre-empt the competition. This involves securing the key tactical as well as key strategic ground and is thus a critical principle of warfare. It means seeing opportunities and threats *before* the competition and then taking the right action to exploit our superior knowledge.

When the environmental changes become full-blown and discernible by the competition, it will be too late for them. In the panic that will ensue, many will lose their previous strengths, thus increasing the opportunities available to those who have already secured the high ground.

Proactive management results in an ability to act coolly and rationally while the competition is in a state of comparative disarray and chaos. Being proactive means having the information *early*. Timeliness, as in warfare, is critical to secure maximum advantage.

The goal of management must thus be to foresee problems and to act to avoid them; **to prevent, not cure**.

The Japanese invest more time in researching, analysing, planning and designing systems and solutions. Their wealth of experience and knowledge, coupled with their dynamic use of technology, has led to improved efficiency. This is the basis of their legendary creativity and ability to get things right first time – and better every time.

Contrary to popular misconception, the Japanese are highly cautious and believe in making decisions by consensus. Consensus should not be confused with decision making by permission. Their aggression does not alter their profound distaste for unnecessary mistakes. Avoidable mistakes result in loss of face – a most serious and undesirable consequence. Having thoroughly eliminated as many of the avoidable obstacles as possible – prior to implementation –

12

the speed of implementation and the resulting success can be mind-boggling. Mistakes are thus made on paper, on the computer screen, and in prototypes rather than in the implemented form.

The best Japanese organisations exemplify Benjamin Franklin's words when he said, 'He that can have patience, can have what he will.'

This aspect of the Japanese mentality explains the seemingly (but deceptive) tedious and unnecessary sluggishness of their decision-making processes.

As Franz Kafka once remarked:

> *All human error is impatience, a premature renunciation of method, a delusive pinning down of a delusion.*

As we will see in Chapter 6, Sun Tzu highlights what he calls 'method and discipline' as one of the five constants that determine success or failure.

As any athlete of worth knows, the more thorough the preparation and warm up, the better one is likely to perform – and with fewer injuries.

Innovative: it is myopic to delegate innovation to only one department (such as R&D or Quality Control). Innovation, change, and constant improvement are the responsibilities of everyone.

Innovation means using existing concepts, tools and methods to solve new problems, or in new applications.

Like most skills, innovativeness must be acquired. This means going onto a learning curve. Learning cannot happen without making the odd mistake. Therefore, if managers are serious about improvement, they will encourage and take

13

practical steps to stimulate learning. Patience and the recognition that genuine mistakes must happen (and, thus, should not be punished) are crucial prerequisites which should be seriously cultivated.

Training and good supervision are vital to generating learning and a reduction in the frequency and impact of mistakes.

The above four characteristics distinguish the champions from the 'also-rans'. Discipline is the fertiliser to achieve their full development. Like all other critical strategic success factors, discipline has to begin from the top – and this must be visible to all.

> *Manoeuvring with an army is advantageous; with an undisciplined multitude, most dangerous.*
>
> Sun Tzu.

Truly great champions are made great by their commitment and discipline.

The Role of Top Management

Top management's primary responsibilities are twofold:

First, to establish the destination (the ultimate strategic goal) that the organisation should be aiming for.

Second, to chart and then steer the corporate ship along a clearly defined route which:

- leads to the desired destination;
- is efficient in terms of scarce resources such as time, fuel, labour, customer comfort etc;
- does not expose the vessel and those on board to risks that should be avoided.

The role of top management should be to set the course (i.e. the direction) that the organisation should take, fully taking into account the opportunities and threats of the various external environments, as well as the strengths and weaknesses of the organisation and its allies (e.g. suppliers and distributors).

Top management should focus strategically on doing *the right things*.

Consider the following parable:

A man decided to become a woodman. He went to the local hardware store and bought the shiniest and sharpest axe available. With this axe he managed to chop down twenty trees a day. After a while, as his axe grew blunt, he was managing to chop down only ten trees a day and he had to work longer hours to do so.

One day, worried by his evident fatigue, the woodman's wife asked him, 'Why don't you sharpen your axe?'

Wearily, her husband replied, 'I don't have time. I am too busy chopping down trees'.

Many of us, in our own ways, are like the foolish woodman.

Much of a typical manager's time is spent on *urgent* matters rather than those that are *important*.

'Urgent' is defined by the Concise Oxford Dictionary as: 'pressing, calling for immediate action or attention'. 'Important' is defined as: 'carrying with it great consequence'.

The more of the important things we have left undone, the more we will spend our time doing urgent things. For example, salespeople spend too much time trying to achieve new sales. This is because they do not spend enough time and effort strengthening existing links, that is, developing goodwill with existing customers.

Remember: if the thing we are doing is not right, then it is probably not worth doing well.

In a useful analogy, top management may be likened to the head, which contains the eyes. The eyes see into the distance. The head also contains the brain. The brain, being fed information by the eyes, transmits messages along the spine.

The spine not only holds the body in place and enables it to function, but also relays messages from the brain to other parts of the body.

Middle (operational) management can be likened to the spine; supervisory management to the arms and legs; and the workforce to the hands and feet.

To say that it all begins with a vision is, therefore, certainly true; as with the body, it is the brain, that begins and manages the entire movement process.

Consequently, the responsibility of the head (management), as principal custodian of the brain (vision), is great; without it, how can life be sustained?

Mismanagement

The majority of company failures result from mismanagement – especially when top management decides on the wrong (or too many) activities.

The reason for this phenomenon is that managers frequently fail to prioritise correctly. I have come across numerous companies where the management is completely oblivious to what business they really ought to be in. As a consequence, they take on activities for which they are ill equipped and neglect those on which they should be concentrating.

It is always tempting to cut corners and go for short-term, fast-route methods to success. Impatience blights the soul of many an entrepreneur and manager. No matter how tempting diversification may seem, there are probably as many businesses that have collapsed as a result of over-extension (through over-diversification) than for any other reason.

The result of wrong priorities? Constant fire-fighting, i.e. managing crises which, like fires, break out because the vital strategic steps, like fire prevention measures, were not taken.

Crisis management forces management to devote increasing amounts of time to short-term issues (problems and symptoms), to the detriment of their vital strategic duties. It is like when a fire breaks out on board a ship. If everybody, including the captain, panics and concentrates all his effort on putting out the fire, nobody will notice the iceberg looming before the ship!

In essence, management should always seek to:

- do the right things,
- in the right way,
- at the right time,
- for the right reasons.

Such an achievement does not come about from chance; diligence and commitment are required.

Conclusion

Develop and maintain power. Knowledge is power. Thus, research and constantly monitor:

1. *The Prize*: our target customers:

   - Why have we targeted this customer group?
   - Is this selection optimal in view of our relative (to competitors) strengths, weaknesses, opportunities, and threats?
   - What are the customers' relevant characteristics?
   - What are the needs we are seeking to satisfy (i.e. what is important to the customer and what is he actually buying)?
   - Is the customer population growing or diminishing?
   - Is the demand per customer increasing?
   - Is there potential for other products and services?
   - How open to influence is the customer?

2. *The Terrain and the Enemy*: examine the relevant external environment, both domestic and international, for opportunities and threats including:

   - economic factors;
   - political stability and country risk;
   - fiscal (tax) changes;
   - industrial relations and labour laws;
   - financing (especially sources and cost of finance);
   - suppliers;
   - distributors;
   - availability and quality of workforce;
   - technological (information, logistics and production) developments;
   - competitors.

3. *Ourselves*: (from the perspectives of the customer and our competitors):

   - What are our strengths and competences?
   - What are our weaknesses, vulnerabilities and dependencies?
   - Consequently, what are our critical success factors?

18

- What is, and what should be, our unique selling proposition (USP), that key strength and advantage which causes our target customers to see us as being the best?

The answers to the above questions will often be highly interactive. For example, our strengths and weaknesses will be dependent on our choice of target customer. Consequently, any change in the choice of target customer may well result in a totally revised list of strengths and weaknesses.

Any temptation to be superficial in analysis must be avoided. 'Text-book' answers may pass business school exams, but to a business aspiring for superiority in the real world, the analysis must penetrate into knowledge that the 'enemy' will not be able to fathom. The initiated will know when they have reached this stage of wisdom when the 'big picture' becomes clear – and when this clarity of vision makes evident the overall strategy that will generate genuine effectiveness and productivity.

All men can see the individual tactics necessary to conquer, but almost no one can see the strategy out of which total victory is evolved.

Sun Tzu.

Develop a **vision**, translate this into a dynamic **mission statement**, then complement these with a **culture statement**.

Educate, inspire and inflame everyone in the organisation with the vision, the mission and the culture.

Maintain the vision and mission through the development, use and management of short-term goals which are translated from the long-term goals (vision). Although initiation is from the top, a 'top-down' approach is not as flexible, and does not work as well in practice, as a 'top-down-iterative' approach. This simply means that top management is receptive to feedback from the divisions (the 'down' elements). If the grassroot feedback indicates that our vision and long-term plans are not feasible or, indeed, are sub-optimal, then they should be reviewed and, if desirable, altered. The approach is, thus, dynamic and iterative.

Remember: it is not possible to inflame others unless you are yourself 'on fire'.

2

STRATEGIC MANAGEMENT THINKING

Let us get one thing clear first of all: Strategic Management Thinking (SMT) is not some new and untested way of thinking. The way one thinks determines the way one works – and the way one works determines the results. This is common sense.

Consequently, both winning and losing begin in our minds. In the previous chapter we saw how champions invest more time and effort in analysis and planning to ensure that avoidable problems *are* avoided. Thus, they achieve levels of productivity that others can only dream about.

The basis of SMT is thinking before acting.

What is SMT?

While few organisations can influence external environmental factors such as politics, inflation, exchange rates and international affairs, these factors will invariably influence the way that businesses operate. Consequently, SMT begins 'outside-in' by investigating the factors (i.e. stimuli) which bring about or inhibit change. Only after this first phase do we consider the entity which will be affected by the change.

SMT prescribes that action is withheld until we have seen the 'big picture'. Seeing the 'big picture' means that we have an overview of our relevant operating environment and any likely changes in it in the foreseeable future. With this awareness, and an understanding of our own strengths and weaknesses (both existing and potential), we are then able to identify core strategic activities where we should concentrate our resources. In this way we can minimise waste and plan away the need for fire-fighting.

The SMT approach is thus characterised by a clear emphasis on being forward looking. However, the key to being forward looking is to recognise that history need not always repeat itself. Additionally, it must also be recognised that even the best laid plans and most thoroughly developed forecasts can go wrong. Contingency planning and the practice of prudence must therefore be an integral part of SMT.

As opportunities and threats undergo radical change, and as our strengths and weaknesses alter, so our strategic focus may also have to be adapted. Decisions, especially strategic ones, must thus be tested by asking how well they will position us in our chosen markets, not only today, but also tomorrow.

The value of superior strategic information cannot be exaggerated. As Sun Tzu puts it:

It is only the enlightened ruler and the wise general who will use the highest intelligence available for spying, and through this they achieve great victories. Spies are vital in war, for the ability of an army to manoeuvre is dependent upon them.

Market research, technical R&D, and databases are to modern businesses what spies are to the military.

'IT IS ONLY THE ENLIGHTENED RULER AND THE WISE GENERAL WHO WILL USE THE HIGHEST INTELLIGENCE AVAILABLE FOR SPYING AND THROUGH THIS THEY ACHIEVE GREAT VICTORIES. SPIES ARE VITAL TO WAR, FOR THE ABILITY OF AN ARMY TO MANOEUVRE IS DEPENDENT UPON THEM '

Information that is unstructured is seldom capable of providing profound knowledge and advantage to the decision maker. He must see each piece of information as a part of a jigsaw. His initial challenge is to fit the pieces together so that his insight is complete. Time and effort must be invested to achieve this.

Insight based on superior use of information is the basis of effective preparation. Preparation must be sufficiently thorough, so that when action is taken, victory will be swift. Timing is always a vital ingredient.

The leader who has grown wise because he has learnt from his experience, and that of others, will realise the profound simplicity of strategies.

Ability to manage circumstances and exact maximum reward is based on the understanding of the core principles of success. Champion strategists go a step further. Instead of considering individual principles in isolation, they are able to create powerful and unfathomable strategies and tactics which are born of the synergistic combination of several of these principles.

Let us illustrate the above concept with an example. Consider the following principles:

- The greatest asset is an excellent reputation.
- Money is power.
- Haste makes waste.
- Patience will bring its own reward.

The above principles, when combined, explain much of the success enjoyed by the truly prosperous. The logic goes as follows:

1. An excellent reputation results in respect and trust from others. The better the reputation, the greater the trust that others will be willing to commit.

24

2. In business, and in life, recurring business and serious investments will come about only when customers and investors have faith in the supplier or business concerned. Greater revenues will result as a business's reputation grows. Profitability will also rise as economies of scale and lower cost of financing (because of the lower risk associated with enhanced reputation and superior performance) are achieved.

3. As assets and creditworthiness increase, the business will attain greater power to move swiftly and to clear obstacles.

4. As the business continues to improve and achieve greater returns on its investments, its reputation will be further enhanced.

5. Excellent reputations can disappear overnight. Impulsiveness and arrogance are common causes. Maintaining the virtue of patience and avoiding haste are keys to the continued strengthening of the most vital asset: one's reputation.

The above cycle can be maintained. This is evident from a brief glance at the top businesses in developed countries. Many of those who were at the top a decade or two ago are still at the top. There are, of course, those who have been toppled, but of these the majority succumbed because they allowed decay to set in. These are the ones who lost what made them great in the first place: their vision and aggression. In their arrogance, they became complacent and careless, and thus unfit and incapable of leading.

As far as core principles are concerned, there are few. Principles are natural laws so, like the seasons, they are unchanging. The expressions and manifestations of natural principles may change, but the underlying principles do not. In understanding this concept, consider the five basic human *needs*:

- physical;
- security;
- social;
- recognition;
- self-realisation.

These have remained unchanged since ancient times. Yet *wants*, which are manifestations (sometimes very confused expressions) of needs, have transformed with every new invention, improvement, and innovation.

In view of this, changes must be carefully monitored and related to the constants, so that the evolving 'big picture' can be seen with clarity. The aim must be to see a trend before our competitors do – and to exploit it to the full.

As *The Art of War* states:

> *Knowing in advance the place and time of the coming battle, we may plan from the greatest distances in order to secure victory.*

Without constant improvement in knowledge and skills, constant improvement is absolutely impossible. Consequently, it is saddening to note that in times of hardship and recession, 'invisibles' (including R&D, market research, information technology, advertising, and customer service) are often the first categories of expenditure to be attacked. It is in bad times that the wise increase such expenditure, knowing full well that their competitors will be doing the exact opposite. The winners extend their lead in difficult times by leveraging the backwardness of their competitors.

From the above it should be evident that effective SMT results not from superior intellect alone: it is dependent also on the quality of information that is processed and the decisiveness of the leadership. Thus, while investment in time, effort, and resources is needed to develop a strategically-oriented organisational culture, such investment enables an organisation to:

- see strengths, weaknesses, opportunities and threats that others are unaware of;
- turn the threats and weaknesses into opportunities and strengths;
- manoeuvre faster and more effectively to secure early success.

Great Japanese companies like Honda and Sony, who have gone from being mere *beneficiaries* of market changes to *engineers* of such change, are experts at SMT. They are living proof that while research and planning should be thorough and conclusive, implementation should be swift and error-free.

To economise foolishly on intelligence and on the quality of personnel is false economy indeed.

> *To remain in ignorance of the enemy's condition, simply because one grudges the cost of the information, is the height of inhumanity. One who behaves in such a manner is of no value to his ruler, and will not attain victory. What enables the wise ruler and great general to strike and conquer, and to achieve results that ordinary men cannot aspire to, is foreknowledge.*
>
> Sun Tzu.

Gathering knowledge and being intimately conversant with new markets is often a good reason for developing alliances. On alliances, Sun Tzu has the following advice to give:

> *We cannot enter into alliances unless we are acquainted with the designs of our [prospective allies]. We are not fit to lead an army unless we are familiar with the terrain. We shall be unable to turn natural advantages to our benefit unless we make use of local guides.*

The theme that knowledge is power underpins this chapter.

Strategy and Tactics

Some people are confused over the concepts of strategy and tactics.

Strategy refers to top-level, long-term plans that influence the entire organisation. Strategy is not encumbered by details of actual day-to-day implementation. Through strategy, we perceive the general direction and are able to justify our choice of methods and tactics to achieve long-term objectives.

Tactics, on the other hand, refer to day-to-day, task-oriented (detailed) activities. Tactics address the question: How do we implement strategy? By no means does this imply that tactics are less important than strategies, or that tactics cannot apply to the entire organisation – they often do (if not directly, then indirectly via the 'domino' effect on products in the same product-range or under the same brand name). Take, for example, advertising campaigns. An individual advertisement is tactical. But who would say that Coca Cola's advertisements are not an integral part of its marketing strategy?

Discussions as to which is more important, strategy or tactic, are merely academic and pointless. It is a chicken-or-egg question that distracts more than enlightens.

What is essential to understand is that tactics are (or, rather, should be) developed from strategies. Do not forget that all strategies must be developed with an eye on practicality and implementability. If they are developed without concomitantly considering whether they are feasible, then it is highly likely that the development exercise will end up being an utter waste of time and resources.

Any strategy must – and this is crucial – be developed with *implementation* (i.e. tactics) in mind.

Benefits of SMT

With conscientious practice, SMT can help management to profitably exploit the very same changes that wreak havoc on the competition.

The principal practical benefits are:

- longer product life-cycle (by being the first, or among the first, to identify and exploit the opportunity);
- faster and greater certainty in recovering initial costs and achieving early profits (by exploiting the demand or skimming the market prior to the build-up of competition);
- greater efficiency and productivity (i.e. superior returns with lower costs and wastage) in resource scheduling and control (as these are planned for in advance);
- less fire-fighting and crisis management (i.e. fewer mistakes as the majority of these will have been identified at the planning stage);
- better feedback and learning as the time spent by others fire-fighting will be used by the champions in systematic monitoring, post-mortems, and design improvement;
- improved teamwork and *esprit de corps* as workers develop a progressive team culture based on sharing success instead of being preoccupied with blaming others for mistakes.

Innovation and superior positioning result from turning what competitors see as threats into opportunities. The most golden of opportunities are frequently the most dangerous of threats – as perceived by the competition. However, in order to successfully exploit this principle, one has to be well prepared and positioned to move decisively at the proper time. Embarking on reckless forays without thorough planning and logistical preparation is like going to war without first gathering intelligence, preparing battle plans, or ensuring that both men and provisions are adequate to secure victory.

Consider how the Japanese car manufacturers exploited the oil crisis in the mid-1970's to their advantage, and to the detriment of the American car 'majors', Ford, GM and Chrysler. In the two years to mid-1992, Japan's share of the US (new) car market soared from 26% to 37% (while Europe's plummeted from 33% to 23%).

Conversely, the greatest opportunities (as seen at the present time) may actually be dire threats. One must avoid making decisions and taking action in haste. Impulsiveness is a very dangerous flaw that has sunk many an entrepreneur.

Ego should be controlled in decision making. Lord King of British Airways was angered when Virgin was allowed into Heathrow. It is said that, in his petulance, he referred to Richard Branson, the chairman of Virgin, as a 'pirate'. This not only inspired Branson in his mission to unseat British Airways as 'The World's Favourite Airline', but also gave him much public sympathy – and free advertising. The same impulsive move also cost Lord King, and British Airways, credibility.

Impulsiveness often results in injury – both direct in the sense that one is weakened, and indirect, as the enemy is strengthened.

To test ideas and proposals (and their real threats and opportunities) systematic common sense should be applied. Ask questions such as: 'If it is really such a great opportunity, why hasn't someone else exploited it?', or 'What are the real costs of failure in the short, medium and long term – and to me personally?'.

Do not accept the assumptions and confident assertions of others, especially those trying to sell an idea to you. They may be sincere but they may also be sincerely wrong. Be enthusiastic once you have accepted a project or proposal but be cautious and thorough in your analysis before doing so. Do this even at the risk of appearing cynical.

Cool-headedness is essential for clear reasoning. Enlisting the help of someone who is sensible and impartial – a devil's advocate – will add to the integrity of the testing and analysis.

Remember: All that glitters is not gold!

Barriers to SMT

Lack of lateral thinking
Sometimes the 'head' decides to look in only one direction. Instead of seeing the full 360-degree picture, only part of it is actually seen. This means that, for top management, the information considered is insufficient: it is like focusing on only one piece of a jigsaw puzzle and failing to consider the rest. Consequently, superior opportunities are lost.

Managers who are autocratic and dogmatic are the principal sufferers of blinkered thinking. Blinkered thinking, or the lack of lateral vision, is, regrettably, a common phenomenon at meetings. The person with the loudest voice, or who happens to be the most aggressive, is usually the one who dominates. Other views are suppressed because the others are often too intimidated (or too concerned about what this will do to the length of the meeting) to contribute or debate.

Thus, at the end of the day, only one point of view is heard and sadly, right or wrong, that is the one that is adopted.

Chairpersons should be skilled and conscientious facilitators. They should ensure that:

- discipline prevails;
- everybody participates;
- there is no monopoly by one or two people (especially if they hold the same views).

In designing strategies, solutions, policies and the like, **genuine participation** is essential if all relevant perspectives are to be taken into account. Also, people are far less inclined to accept and use what they have not been involved in designing or developing. Consider what would happen if important perspectives (e.g. of trades unions) were omitted: policies, no matter how logical, would be rejected. In addition, deteriorating industrial relations, demoralisation, and falling productivity could be triggered off as well.

Genuine participation radically improves the likelihood of successful implementation of solutions.

Participation works because:

- it satisfies the basic need for recognition;
- it is vital to understanding and learning; the experience and knowledge of how the system works will also enable the users to remedy problems and introduce improvements;
- the result (be it a decision, a system, or a policy, etc.) will be 'owned' by the users who will then feel morally responsible for the successful operation of the system they helped to create.

For participation to work fully, we have to ensure that:

- there is clear and adequate delegation (this means responsibility, accountability, and authority);
- the ultimate 'owner' of the decision area (the person who has the power to decide on the matter without reference to any higher authority) is genuinely committed to the results and communicates this

effectively and practically to those expected to participate;

- the participation is genuine and not manipulative: people detest being manipulated, and sooner or later they will realise the deception;
- speedy and accurate feedback is given, preferably built-in as part of the system; without this, enthusiasm and continuity will peter out.

Lateral thinking is achieved by, among other things, not rejecting suggestions without adequate consideration. Let us consider a practical application of this principle: during 'brainstorming' sessions (which are a vital part of such creative processes), no suggestion should be rejected. Every suggestion should be recorded for discussion during the second phase of the session. The first phase of brainstorming is an unstructured process of generating and gathering ideas; this has nothing to do with selection and rejection!

Ideas which may appear stupid on first hearing, may be great ideas which have been poorly put across. These 'silly' ideas, when explored further, can result in **serendipity**: the making of happy and unexpected discoveries by accident. Serendipity leads to richer insight. It is amazing how often this happens, and how beneficial such sessions can be, not only in developing direct solutions, but in developing interpersonal and communications skills, and in improving team spirit and cooperation.

Lateral thinking may thus be defined as seeing hidden realities and solutions. This ability is a hallmark of successful innovators.

Management myopia
This refers to the fixation many western managers have with short-term issues at the expense of long-term, strategic considerations.

One reason why managers prefer dealing with short-term matters is that they are not trained to think strategically. Consider the opportunity cost of ignoring long-term or wider considerations.

Most Japanese businesses use as their key performance measure the ultimate strategic criterion: market share. Compare this to the two main indicators favoured by British companies: ROCE (return on capital employed) and EPS (earnings per share), both of which are essentially short-term measures.

Before continuing, we need to be clear about one thing: short-term criteria, in particular cash flow and profit, *are* vital considerations. This is beyond dispute. What needs to be understood, however, is that strategy should always seek to accommodate both long-term and short-term essentials. Any strategy should thus provide for survival as well as for profitable expansion (ideally with reduced risk). To sacrifice the long term in favour of short-term interests would be tantamount to chopping off the head of the goose that lays golden eggs!

Take, for example, cost cutting exercises by managers to maximise short-term profits – to secure promotion, perhaps. They might achieve impressive cost reductions through neglecting customer service, plant maintenance, research and development, training or advertising. Consider the impact of these actions on the organisation's ability to weather the storm of competition (or cash-flow) beyond the short term.

Much of the blame for management myopia can be laid at the doors of the shareholders, lenders, and investment analysts. These, in general, appear to suffer from 'obsession with numbers'. Both in the US and in Europe, too few seem able to see beyond the (current) 'bottom line'.

34

While profits are, indisputably important, many profitable businesses still become insolvent.

Business failure frequently results from an inability to manage cash flows. In such cases the timing and volume of cash inflows do not match cash outflows. Situations leading to this outcome fall into two categories:

Overtrading: where purchases need to be paid for earlier than the receipt of sales proceeds (especially common in times of rapidly rising inflation);

Overgearing: where the cost of servicing debt (interest and capital repayments, for example) is unmanageable. This situation is especially endemic during periods which are marked by high interest rates and economic recession.

Where short-term criteria are used as the main measures of performance, bankers (who have their own bosses and shareholders to account to) become all too quick to pull the rug from under businesses which are undergoing difficult times. In doing so, many viable businesses go to the wall unnecessarily – and the economy becomes further depressed.

Another consequence of valuing and rating businesses (almost solely) on their short-term performance, is that companies in turn appraise and reward their managers on the basis of equally short-term yardsticks. Thus, in defence of the managers who behave sub-optimally, can they be blamed if they are rewarded precisely for such behaviour?

Let us remind ourselves of the LeBouef Principle:

We get more of the behaviour we reward.

Bottom-up (inside-out) Management

Instead of using the top-down (outside-in) approach, managers who are neither trained nor rewarded to think or behave strategically, tend to work in reverse!

I meet managers who tell me, 'I'm a practical person'. These words never fail to fill me with a sense of dread. In many cases, the self-acclaimed *practical* manager is one who suffers from inertia, and who resists change (because change may expose weaknesses) and any use of time to consider broader and longer-term consequences and needs. It often seems that all such managers are interested in are schedules (but not clearly defined milestone objectives) and costs (but not targeted benefits, including those affecting other areas of the operation or those which will be evident only in the longer term).

These managers are usually also the same people who see things in black and white and who expect proposals to be correct first time, without spending any time or effort on fact-finding and research. They spend too much time reviewing and rejecting opportunities, rather than refining those with potential and making them work.

Their argument is that we should all be 'pragmatic'. By this, they mean that we should only concentrate on dealing with the things that are happening here (in the company and with our existing customers), and now (i.e. forget the future). Such an attitude implies that what is happening in the outside world (in our relevant external environments, which will impact on our markets, customers and operations) can be ignored. This is nothing short of suicide!

Two of Sun Tzu's five constant factors which govern the art of war are **Heaven** and **Earth**. In the context of business, Heaven represents the environmental factors (opportunities and threats) which normally cannot be controlled (like seasonal fluctuations in demand and supply, natural disasters, politics, fiscal policy), whilst Earth symbolises the terrain of the battlefield (the size of the population, fashion trends, barriers to entry, distribution costs, competitors).

If a business is to be truly market-driven and proactive (which it must be to survive), then there is no way it can afford to manage without a knowledge of *Heaven and Earth*.

The following message has been adapted from an excellent article which appeared in the *International Herald Tribune*:

> Pragmatism . . . a day at a time, a problem at a time.
> But pragmatism has its limits.
> Without a vision, and public understanding of it,
> policy cannot meet long-range needs . . .
> least of all at a time of fundamental change.
> Every once in a while, (we) need to set a course.
> This is such a time!

Managers and organisations who hide behind the excuse of 'being pragmatic' are blind to the fact that the world is changing and, unless they adapt, they will suffer the fate of the dinosaur.

Strategic Information

If an organisation is to survive the turbulence that is even now escalating, it must be information strong.

Being information strong does not mean having masses of information. If information is the lifeblood of an organisation, having too much of it may result in pressure greater than the vessels and organs can bear. Haemorrhaging can be fatal. Too much of a good thing can be a bad thing.

The secret is *quality* and *value*, as defined by the user; not quantity.

As information becomes cheaper and the sources proliferate, managers are becoming inundated with information that they 'cannot afford to do without'. Information overload, together with untailored, unfocused and poorly presented material, is a serious cause of management inefficiency in many organisations I have personally come across.

Especially for senior management, information needs to be condensed; this enables the senior executive to grasp the overall scenario without becoming distracted by excessive detail and minutiae. A key benefit of good presentation and tailoring of information is that managers are saved time that they would otherwise have to spend manipulating and analysing the data presented, and then searching for additional information. The time saved could be far more productively invested in interpretation, decision making, problem solving, and implementation. Modern Executive Information Systems (EIS), using state-of-the-art technologies such as artificial intelligence, are designed to achieve this benefit.

Strategic information systems must enable the organisation to:

- identify relevant changes before they happen;
- plan to minimise the downside of, and to exploit, the changes at the right time and cost-effectively;
- react quickly and effectively to changes that could not have been foreseen;
- measure the results of activities for effective control and to sustain improvement.

The design of any information system must reflect the fact that timing is crucial for effective and proactive management. In practice many reports are prepared and disseminated at given intervals. This may reduce the value of the information. For example, in project management, different activities may be interdependent. In such cases, if the results of earlier activities are not relayed speedily, later activities may be adversely affected, leading to sub-optimal results overall.

The great organisations of today and tomorrow are, and will remain, those who are superior in the management and exploitation of information.

Information should always be:

- timely (and swift);
- accurate;
- comprehensive;
- relevant: non-relevant information (noise) can distract and lead to sub-optimal decisions;
- actionable – this involves not only content, but clarity, format, logic and user-friendliness of presentation.

The Comprehensive Analysis Programme

Avoidable risk is unhealthy. Plans and solutions should therefore be flexible and capable of delivering good results under a wide range of possible situations. Such robustness is necessary as the future is becoming increasingly difficult to predict with any degree of accuracy.

Conglomerates, for example, seek diversification as a way of achieving *synergy*. Synergy adds value to the group as a whole. In other words, the whole is worth more than the sum of its parts. A crucial aspect of synergy in this concept is the reduction of overall risk.

When we talk about risk, we are really talking about the uncertainty of future outcomes. Risk can thus be reduced through improving certainty. To do so, a better picture of the future is needed. Consequently, forecasts of the future states of both external (uncontrollable) and internal (more controllable) factors which influence performance need to be undertaken.

Most Pessimistic	Most Likely	Optimistic

INTERACTING PERSPECTIVES OF:
(Domestic and Global)

Customers (buyers, users
and gatekeepers)
Financiers
Owners
Competitors
Suppliers
Distributors
Employees
Managers
Employers
Interest Groups (e.g.
ecology groups)
Governments
Consultants (e.g. lawyers,
accountants, management consultants)
General Public
Others

Diagram: COMPREHENSIVE ANALYSIS PROGRAM (CAP)

I developed the Comprehensive Analysis Programme (CAP) as a framework for developing and testing decisions, systems and solutions, by looking at as many relevant external and internal (Heaven and Earth) factors as feasible. To do this we

40

try to involve the various parties listed in the CAP, or endeavour to view the problem, our analysis, and possible solutions, from their perspectives. This can be exceedingly hard to do if we are not thoroughly familiar with the mentalities of the parties concerned. The disciplined use of the model will result in solutions that are robust and holistic. Additionally, solutions developed in this way are likely to be substantially less vulnerable to deficiencies which result from lack of insight, or from omitting some important perspective.

In using CAP, the parties involved should be segregated into **primary**, the main influencers, and **secondary**. In some less developed countries, business success is a function of how much influence the business has over the political strongmen or their spouses and close relatives. The latter would thus be categorised as primary.

Within the primary category, it is also advisable to rank the parties, according to the situation at hand. Consider, for example, the following case: a national marketing programme is being developed to attract foreign investors. Obviously, the target investors would become the prime focus (in this case as the customer). Such a programme must identify and address the priority concerns that such investors are likely to have, for example:

- political stability and country risk;
- workforce: skills and industrial relations;
- operational efficiency and costs (especially taxation, and sophistication of infrastructuring: transportation and communications in particular).

The aim of the marketing programme may be to achieve substantial inflow of funds from targeted investors within a given time period. For the objective to be achieved, the 'product' must itself be attractive to the target customers (investors and gatekeepers) and also be capable of standing

41

up to scrutiny. This means that the product must be designed, developed, and guaranteed. This cannot be achieved effectively without the practical commitment of key parties – especially relevant ministries. They must be willing to commit themselves to changes and provisions which meet the needs of foreign investors and their key gatekeepers.

It should be evident that the practices, attitudes and policies of all those able to influence the target investor's behaviour should be thoroughly researched. Examples of such influencers include:

- the Ministries of Finance, Economy, Trade and Industry;
- trade unions;
- competitors (domestic and foreign);
- chambers of commerce;
- banks;
- professional advisors;
- employees (expats and their families).

It is also vital to note that the analysis must probe beyond what presently exists. Our knowledge must also reflect forecasts of future changes and scenarios.

CAP is based on **Scenario Analysis**. Ideally, at least two or three different scenarios should be considered. In practice, the two most important scenarios are: the worst possible outcome; and the most likely outcome.

In applying CAP, the first step is to identify the possible scenarios which exist in the future. Systems and solutions which will operate well under those given scenarios may then be developed. By using scenario analysis, the potential risks are identified (depending, of course, on the quality of the input data) and assessed with reference to the decision maker's degree of risk aversion (or risk tolerance).

42

By consciously recognising that various states of the future are possible, the approach helps to develop robust, flexible and implementable solutions. A more realistic view of the problem will result.

It must be emphasised that this approach must be **forward looking**. This means that systems (or solutions) must be designed to meet needs that will exist when the system is actually implemented or which will arise thereafter. Some of these may not be needs which exist at the present. Examples of such needs include:

- rapid order processing;
- acceptance of new forms of payment (such as credit cards);
- real-time communication between databases situated in various parts of the globe.

Thus systems need to be effective (and state-of-the-art) when they go 'live', not necessarily at the time of design or trial. It is unproductive to develop solutions that are good now, but obsolete when actually implemented.

Consequently, likely changes before the implementation date must be taken into account. Naturally, this will depend on the cost and gravity of the project or decision concerned. Should a project be substantial and/or require a lengthy design and development period, cutting cost and effort in this crucial, 'upfront' aspect of the analysis would indeed be pursuing false economies; it will almost invariably lead to higher costs (including opportunity costs), loss of productivity, increased frustration and fire-fighting.

The CAP may thus be described as 'front-end weighted'. Its main value is that, owing to its logical and non-technical orientation, it can be applied to and improve almost any form of decision making, problem solving, or system development.

Conclusion

We need to:

- **Be knowledge strong**

It is necessary to keep abreast of relevant developments and to deepen our understanding of which are the key factors and how these interact to influence performance and results. Information Technology should be exploited to achieve productivity. This need not be expensive, as long as the total organisation is geared (trained and rewarded) for information and communication. This stimulates the learning curve – especially as IT systems drop in price.

Even if costly, consider the question, can we (not only in the short term) afford to do without superior intelligence?

Although I have quoted these lines from Sun Tzu before, they are so profound that they are worth noting again here:

> *Hostile armies may confront each other for years, striving for the victory that is decided in a single day. This being the case, to remain ignorant of the enemy's position, strengths and weaknesses, simply because one grudges the outlay of a sum of money, is the height of inhumanity (and shortsightedness).*

This principle can and should be applied to every aspect of business and leadership. But, let common sense prevail. Make use of rich and effective (but often cheap) sources of data such as salespeople, trade journals, newspaper articles, chambers of commerce, government statistics, customer surveys, samples of competitors' products, visits to distributors, street surveys, foot counts, etc. From experience, commercial and trade departments of embassies tend to be poor sources of information – except the very basic.

Once obtained, the data should be skilfully processed and presented so as to motivate the users to actually use them. With the availability of affordable but sophisticated and user-friendly systems, managers and other users are able to tailor reports according to their own needs and wants.

- **Act on information – don't waste it**

Information is power, but only if it is effectively used! Information systems need to motivate championship behaviour!

- **Train and equip managers to think, plan and act strategically**

According to an article in an August issue of *The Economist* in 1991 Japanese car plants in the US invest seven times as much in training than do American plants – and the productivity achieved is many times higher, as a result.

Principle: don't expect anyone to do anything well if he does not know how to do it and/or has not been provided with the right tools.

- **Reward our managers when they behave strategically**

You get more of the behaviour you reward.

- **Build the team – rally the troops!**

Quality motivates! Competition also motivates and helps create the outside pressure that tightens teams. Try keeping people informed about competitors (them) and use this to develop team unity (us). Make everyone in the organisation feel that they really belong and are vital to the 'army'.

- **Don't act before seeing the 'big picture'**

The Japanese set the pace and standard for the rest of the world to follow in many things. Is it not strange that, traditionally, they have never seemed to be in a hurry to implement? Once they do, however, things get done fast – and the success rates are distinctly superior.

To ensure that the 'big picture' we see is the real one, test all key assumptions. Ensure that the picture is complete, with no significant omissions.

Avoid blind faith in information received. If the consequence is serious, verify the information; statistics, in particular, are often manipulated. Question the reliability and validity of the source. With each piece of information received, ask if it is compatible and consistent with existing knowledge. Question the implications and significance, by asking, 'So what? What does this mean in confirming or altering our planned action?'

- **Emulate champions**

The conclusion is clear: start following the right role models – *now*! Seek to equal – and then surpass – the very best! We will achieve only as great as we aspire.

3

THE DEATH OF THE MASS MARKET

The industrial revolution was born of automation.

Automation achieved lower costs (mainly labour and time-related costs) and large standardised volumes of production. This gave rise to the mass markets: not much innovation, but agreeable prices and 'standard' features.

With increasing customer (both industrial and end-consumer) sophistication, the trend is towards:

- greater innovation;
- faster changes in taste and product/service features demanded;
- customised products and services;
- greater choice;
- (the good news) distinct willingness by customers to pay for quality;
- (last, but by no means least) excellence of customer service.

This means that manufacturers and suppliers of goods and services should:

- focus on giving great value to the customer;
- deliver a consistent standard of service excellence that results in customer loyalty;
- shorten response time;
- eliminate waste, inefficient methods, and unproductive activities;
- welcome smaller order-quantities (to cultivate 'acorn' customers and to reduce dependency on large customers).

The shortening of product life cycles is an especially strong tendency in product markets that are driven by innovation. This is certainly the case in consumer electronics. There are signs, however, in other industries, that some manufacturers have gone too far in the frequency with which they introduce new 'improved' models. An example is the family saloon and sports car segments of the car industry. There is an increasingly widespread perception among consumers that Japanese auto manufacturers innovate too frequently, and that models get replaced too often. Not only does this practice increase costs, but it also removes an incentive to purchase, as the model one buys is likely to become 'old' within a couple of years.

In short, businesses must now become increasingly specialised. They must become expert in their chosen segment. By concentrating all their efforts in one segment (or splitting up their organisation into specialist teams), they get to know their market(s) better. By adopting this approach, they will avoid spreading their strengths (resources) over a vast 'general' market.

The trend therefore, is toward becoming a big, healthy fish in a smaller pond (although fishes in different ponds may come from the same family).

... BUSINESSES MUST NOW BECOME INCREASINGLY SPECIALISED.

When we talk about flexibility as a condition for survival, we are referring to Total Flexibility. This encompasses the way we think, the way we deal with clients, environmental changes, competitors, our people and our technology. Nothing is left out: if we did omit anything important, it could very well prove to be our fatal weak link.

It is therefore important to constantly monitor and regularly review our organisation's activity chains, chains which include our allies as well as our internal (operational) activities. Look what happened to a bottler of mineral water a few years back when it was remiss in checking its filters for contamination!

Mass markets are definitely on the rapid decline. Even in banking and financial services, specialist 'boutiques' have taken off, and are already nipping at the heels of established banking names.

See the writing on the wall. Even to the blind, there is no mistaking the message.

It is no longer possible to fool customers with poor products and services, even if these come complete with high budget, glitzy packaging and advertising.

The total marketing strategy must be soundly founded on the concept of Perceived Relative Quality (PRQ – the customer's perception of quality, based on what he needs, wants, values and is willing to pay for, and what is on offer in the market place).

The ultimatum: If we cannot provide our customers with what they want, when they want, then we will lose them to competitors who can and are willing to do so.

With the loss of customers, we lose the opportunity to

THE ULTIMATUM: IF WE CANNOT PROVIDE OUR CUSTOMERS WITH WHAT THEY WANT, WHEN THEY WANT, THEN WE WILL LOSE THEM TO COMPETITORS WHO CAN, AND ARE WILLING TO DO SO.

provide them with more goods and services or increase the sale and profit contribution per customer.

Perceived Relative Quality

More than ever, with increasingly aggressive, high-quality competition, it is necessary to differentiate ourselves and our offerings from our competitors and their products. We must aim not only to *be* positively (favourably) unique, but to be *seen* that way as well – especially by our target customers and key influencers.

To achieve clear differentiation, enlightened companies increasingly seek to 'de-commoditise': to get their customers to view their products as more than *standard* commodities and to convince the customer that their product/service meets his need(s) uniquely.

This is the sole objective of modern marketing: to make what we offer much more appealing to our target customers than any alternative product/service – and in such a way that our goals of profit, growth, market share, social responsibility and employee welfare are achieved.

A marketing adage (originator: Professor Theodore Leavitt) is: *nobody buys a product or service – people only buy solutions to their problems, needs and (increasingly) desires!*

Consequently, one of the first steps to be taken in understanding a customer is to discover what needs (which may even contradict what he thinks he wants) he wishes to fulfil through the purchase.

Maslow's Hierarchy of Needs model (below) is a very powerful and useful tool (though much under-appreciated) for understanding needs and for sharpening focus in product-development strategy.

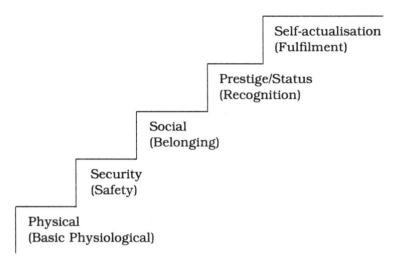

Diagram: Maslow's Hierarchy of Needs

Marketing executives, entrepreneurs, negotiators and salespeople must know clearly not only who their customers are, but also their priority need or needs. The key to success is giving the customer what will meet his underlying needs better than the competitors, and to avoid wasting time and money on features that do nothing to meet those needs. The importance of this critical insight cannot be exaggerated: it is what distinguishes the winners from the rest.

To illustrate with a simple example, cars were originally developed to fulfil a basic physiological need: transportation. A Skoda would fulfil this need. However, a person who buys a Ferrari will not be doing so to satisfy this basic need. A Ferrari, being a status symbol, will be acquired to meet a prestige need.

The Product-Service Compound

Differentiation, even in basic products, can only be achieved on a sustained basis through marketing a compound of a product with a service. No physical product can stand on its own.

Manufacturers and suppliers can no longer afford to think of their business as being merely the *supply* of goods and services. Quality in 'surround' services, especially after-sales and customer service, are becoming established as the hallmarks of superior, market-beating enterprises.

A caveat is needed to round off our discussion on differentiation. We differentiate so as to achieve and sustain competitive advantage. That which makes us, in the eyes of the customer, superior to the competition is called the Unique Selling Proposition (USP). However, it is critical to ensure that the things we are doing to differentiate ourselves do not cause us to move (unless this is planned) into a different market segment – which might be less profitable and/or one in which we have no knowledge or experience. Our actions must be seen by our target customers to add, not take away, value. For example, some Far Eastern T-shirt manufacturers print gaudy 'down-market' designs onto their products. The additional printing costs money, but actually lowers the price of the products because they are perceived to be 'cheap and nasty' (or as they say in England, 'naff').

Conclusion

We must restructure our companies into fast, flexible and flat organisations. However, restructuring, *per se*, is inadequate. The way ahead is through expert teams operating in very clearly defined niche markets.

Our focus, as far as market segment and core businesses are concerned, must be specific and logical, based on an ongoing strengths, weaknesses, opportunities and threats (SWOT) analysis.

To be greedy and attempt to operate more businesses, or in more market segments than we can handle, could damage the effectiveness of our Unique Selling Proposition (USP) and possibly even prove fatal.

Customers are getting more sophisticated, and increasingly want to be serviced by specialists. As such, businesses had better start focusing on appropriate and manageable niches rather than continuing with the 'blunderbuss' approach.

4

TOTAL QUALITY MANAGEMENT

Quality is rated according to how well a service or product fits the expectations, needs and wants of the customer.

Since we aspire to be true champions, we will use words which inspire aspiration beyond the goals of those who would be satisfied with less. Consequently let us define **quality** as: *the degree of excellence by which we delight our customer.*

Quality: The Top Priority

Let us remind ourselves that obsessing the total organisation begins from the top. Acceptance of mediocre performance and mixed standards must be eliminated. No longer will sluggish behaviour and lukewarm quality improvement exercises be tolerated.

Quality is not some vague notion of improvement or 'doing one's best'. Quality means clearly defined and measurable performance based on objective standards. If something 'cannot' be measured, then perhaps the function is irrelevant, and should be eliminated.

Measures that can be used to gauge improvement in quality include:

- number of errors/defects;
- incidence of variation;
- number of customer complaints;
- time taken to perform a duty;
- absenteeism (in person-days);
- increased productivity;
- number of suggestions made which have been implemented.

With reference to the number of defects, errors and complaints, we should aim for a consistent zero.

Taking this one step further, the goal of TQM may be stated even more challengingly as:

to get it right first time, and then better, every time.

As to how to implement TQM and achieve the above goal, the formula is:

kaizen + technological innovation.

Kaizen is the Japanese term meaning '*constant improvement involving everyone*'.

Quality Motivates

Consider the following facts:

- People (contrary to what some bosses may think) are energised and motivated by quality because people inherently *desire* to be challenged and to achieve their best.
- Perceived Relative Quality is the single most important deciding factor governing purchase and re-purchase behaviour (source: TARP).

- Customers are willing to pay more for quality, and lots more for the *best*.
- Businesses which use a marketing strategy based on quality achieve significantly superior profitable growth. In short, they survive, profit, grow and prosper much faster and better than those who compete on some other basis, like price. Companies like Marks and Spencer (which unlike lesser retail giants, still manage to make significant increases in profits even in recessionary times) are living testaments to this truth.
- Quality pays for itself. To quote Bill Cosby, 'Quality is *free!*' The increase in revenues and cost-efficiencies fund any cost involved in setting up a quality programme.

Caveat: As we live in the real world with real world problems, let us be realistic about the scope of considerations covered by the word 'quality'. We must remember that the customer and his expectations are both influenced by circumstances from without and from within (such as economic trends and health).

When we talk about perceived relative quality, we should note the 'relative' in the term. Price must not be forgotten as 'value' (especially in recessionary times, and as sophistication and awareness of alternatives develops) is still an important consideration.

When Rolls Royce had to be nationalised, it was not because the company failed to achieve quality; it made the best engines in the world in those days. The problem was that the engineer-managers failed to remember that their customers had budgets to answer to; beyond a certain point, marginal increments in excellence (at the cost of substantial price increments) became academic and unwarranted.

The Win-Win Situation

Think about it. When do we really do good work and achieve great results? When we are feeling bad about ourselves, or other people? Of course not! We do our best work and get the best output when we feel great! Great about ourselves and about others. When we are at peace with the world, and ready to collaborate. This is called a Win-Win situation.

To ensure that everybody achieves great results (especially as a team), we need to create the Win-Win environment throughout our organisation. Not only is this good for short-term performance, it also builds loyalty and long-term teamwork. People who feel happy do not want to leave! And we know that the longer a team works together, plays together, and generally improves together, the better and stronger the teamwork and bond of camaraderie is likely to become.

Another very important motivation that results from achieving top quality is **pride**: not the self-centred and introverted type, but the type that is dynamic, positive and energising. This type of pride welcomes criticism as a means of adapting to remain the very best! As managers, we must realise (and do something about it!) that a key job is to build up the pride of our team.

Positive pride can be a great way of **differentiating** both our product and service, and thus widen the gulf between ourselves and our competitors, in our favour, of course!

Let me tell you something that happened to me. Just this afternoon I went into the local Superstore to get some ginger and spring onions. The queues were not too bad for a Saturday afternoon, but I spent (wasted!) twenty-five minutes from joining the queue to leaving the store, even though there were only two people ahead of me (and they did not have very much shopping) – and despite the fact that the store was equipped with the most up-to-date computerised salespoint systems.

Why?

To cut a long story short, the symptoms spelt: **inadequate training**. However, the core problem was the attitude – an attitude that began with top management and filtered down to affect every checkout person. Demotivation and low morale were patently evident in the zombie-like manner in which purchases were checked out.

And speed? To quote a statement made by a disgruntled employee in the excellent training video *Who killed the sale*, 'There are two speeds: dead slow and stop!' Not a smile was to be seen on the faces of any of the staff I encountered. While I was waiting for my change (this wait was in excess of fifteen minutes as no supervisor was available to rectify a mistake involving the amount of cash received by the checkout person), I asked one of the managers why the service had deteriorated so badly for it had once been rather good.

His reply was, 'I know it's b––––– bad, I don't shop here myself, I shop at . . . (name of a competing store).'

It's really sad isn't it, when the members of an organisation have no pride or commitment to it? So much so that they would rather travel some six miles away to patronise a competitor.

Is the attitude described above the attitude of our people? If it is, then we must do something urgently to reverse the situation. Negative attitude of this kind is like a very aggressive cancer: it spreads quickly and kills off good and healthy cells.

But how? Let's consider a way of dealing with both the core attitudes (of everyone in the organisation) and the resultant symptoms. Let's look at Total Quality Management (TQM).

What is TQM?

TQM is about building a living armour: flexible, yet impenetrable, and without weak links.

In the legends about great Chinese pugilists, one of the most famous was Fong Sai Yok – a fighter of tremendous skill. Fong, at a very young age, had already attained a high level of development in the art of *Ti Poh Sum*; internal strength (chi) made him virtually invulnerable to blows. Notwithstanding this ability, he was killed in a fight. Fong's fatal contest was with his aunt, Wu Mei, another fighter of great renown. She knew of his single weak point. And when the opportunity availed itself (which she engineered in the course of the fight), she struck that weak point with her most deadly technique – and with deadly precision.

This story highlights five crucial principles of combat:

- know your enemy;
- know yourself;
- know the terrain;
- be prepared and scheme to exploit your knowledge of the conditions – employ the 'divine art' of deception;
- apply your strength against the enemy's weakness.

Sun Tzu states that the excellent general is one who makes himself and his forces **unassailable**. To do this, he

61

THE EXCELLENT GENERAL IS ONE WHO MAKES HIMSELF AND HIS FORCES UNASSAILABLE.

recognises his own weaknesses, not just his strengths. He then ensures that his weaknesses are eliminated, turned into strengths, or covered so well that nothing the enemy does will cause them to be exposed.

TQM is a key to achieving unassailability in business warfare.

To the West, TQM is a relatively recent, dynamic and holistic management approach based on making quality the essential part of an organisation's culture. Although considered a Japanese 'export', strangely enough, it was an American (Dr Edwards Deming) who introduced the basic techniques to the Japanese after the Second World War.

With TQM, quality becomes the driving philosophy and key motivator for everyone.

TQM is initiated by fiery enthusiasm from the very top. It involves everyone seeing himself as a supplier – as well as a customer – to others in his organisation.

And, since the customer is 'boss', everyone gets a chance to be listened to and treated like the boss.

How to implement TQM

Requirements

- Top Management must be inflamed with becoming the very best as seen through the eyes of the customer.
- Through consistent example, training, equipping, rewarding, motivating and concerted teamwork, the fire of quality and becoming the best must be spread to the rest of the organisation. Everyone becomes, and is seen to be, an expert in his own job.
- Uncompromisingly, the passion for quality must be systematically sustained.

Total means just that: everything, every part, and everyone; we are not only talking about great quality of products and services, we are also talking about great productivity leading to demonstrably superior value.

The key steps

1. Top management (the whole board) must personally explain the programme to the entire organisation: memos alone will not do.
2. Each person (this includes the CEO) and every department must identify their 'customers', both internal and external. It is likely that everyone will be both a customer *and* a supplier to other members of the organisation.
3. Customers and suppliers working together must agree on desired improvements and establish measurable performance criteria. These customer-supplier teams should arrange regular reviews, especially at the early stages.

The over-riding objective of these teams will be to achieve maximum benefits for the customer. But what of the supplier?

First, he will be someone else's customer and so will also be receiving 'royal' treatment.

Second, he will welcome the chance to achieve excellence and thereby self-actualise.

Third, the improving team spirit will make his job more enjoyable, thus meeting a social need while at work.

Fourth, he will recognise that **if his team** (including his 'customer') **wins, he wins**.

Fifth, the feedback that he receives from his customer will have tremendous motivational value. The 'customer' of course, will have been well trained in interpersonal skills.

4. An open-communication culture must be developed: different parts of the organisation must talk to develop effective teams. Additionally, other means of communicating what is happening in one part of the organisation to the other divisions and departments, such as a company newsletter, should be developed.
5. Performance should be recorded as soon as possible, in highly visible form (on a signboard located by the workstation, for example), by the performers themselves.
6. A suggestion scheme should be set up and ¡all suggestions considered for implementation. Towards the end of the 1980s, Toyota was receiving in excess of 40,000 employee suggestions; of these, over 95% were actually implemented!
7. Quality Committees (with top management involvement) must be established and trained to oversee and sustain specific quality programmes.
8. Improvements – and failures – must be analysed to understand the causes. This is vital to learning: in this way positive behaviour will be reinforced and negative behaviour reduced.
9. Improvements must be celebrated and rewarded: recognition is a basic human need and motivator. This rewards the positive behaviour we want to reinforce. Again, top management involvement will greatly help to enhance the motivational value of these celebrations.
10. Masaaki Imai, one of the pioneers of modern TQM, says: '*Quality begins with training, and ends with training.*' To skimp on costs by reducing or eliminating training, is to steal from the organisation's future (potential) prosperity.

If the precept that 'people are our critical resource' is a genuine part of an organisation's culture (and not just lip service), then training should be seen as an

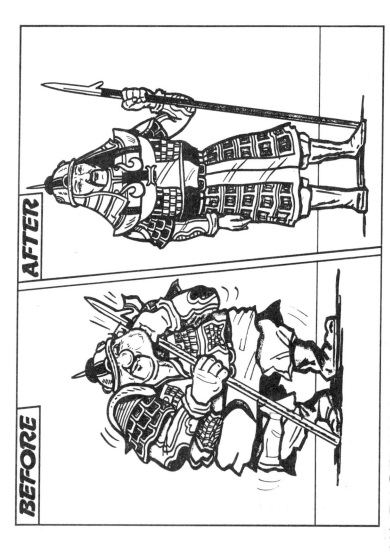

BEFORE

AFTER

QUALITY BEGINS WITH TRAINING AND ENDS WITH TRAINING.

essential investment and commensurate provisions from the budget should be set aside for it. Investment in quality very quickly pays for itself, and also pays rich dividends!

The provision of quality training is also an act of commitment to the individuals and teams involved. Again, this may be a case of loyalty downwards resulting in loyalty upwards.

Failure of Total Quality Programmes

Warning: In the UK, 95% of Total Quality Programmes fail.

Two principal reasons for this distressing phenomenon are:

1. Enthusiasm without a System for Implementation and Control
There is great initial enthusiasm, but because of the lack of training, induction and systematic organisation, failures breed frustration. Before too long, the spark goes out.

2. System without Enthusiasm
This time, the programme is well structured, and monitoring controls are in place, but the positive enthusiasm that is required to ignite the Total Quality fuse is not there.

Because top management passion was missing from the start, the programme doesn't even take off before dying away.

The danger with failure is that it tends to discourage many from re-attempting. As a result, bright prospects are often lost.

What distinguishes the true champions from the 'flash-in-the-pan' winners is the ability to *sustain* success, especially in the face of severe trials and failures. True champions get up and fight on – others just slink away from the arena, never to be heard from again.

It all boils down to attitude. Winning and Quality are both attitudes. Sustaining success depends on tenacity and resilience: great virtues in business, as they are in life.

Networking: The Dynamic Extension of TQM

TQM can be extended beyond the confines of an individual organisation. By linking up with customers and suppliers, great advances and dynamic synergies can be achieved. We are not advocating vertical integrations (which imply equity control), but systematic cooperation and coordination.

Example:

A shirt manufacturer decides that it needs to penetrate domestically as well as to expand into foreign markets. An effective way to increase its credibility (a fuller range of products, better presentation material, for example) while reducing the cost of the foreign marketing, might be to link up its marketing efforts with a suit manufacturer of similar reputation and quality who is targeting the same customer segment.

Together, they may then link up with their material suppliers. In this case, the design and production of material can then be developed with the designers of the shirts and suits, thus achieving better overall design and preparation, and lowering cost through sharing.

Retailers can then place orders directly with the material suppliers. This is a radical departure from the normal practice, whereby the clothing manufacturer receives the order, processes it and then places an order with the supplier. The re-routing of the order means there will be no delay in order processing and production scheduling. This should reduce delivery time and enhance the image of the clothing manufacturers in the eyes of the retailers. Naturally, improved perception of quality will mean improved prices.

Additionally, this new system could be used to launch a Just In Time (JIT) system, which would *inter alia* cut down stock holding costs, improve quality, and reduce the 'fire-fighting' brought about by changes in customer demand or fashion trends.

These are just some of the benefits which such a network could achieve. Each network member as part of an extended team will have constant incentives to improve their quality and efficiency, thus giving rise to a Win-Win relationship.

Notwithstanding the benefits, there will be difficulties in getting different parties with different, and possibly conflicting, cultures to work together in such a radical way. Care must be taken to choose compatible partners and to ensure that politicking and bureaucracy do not result.

The systematic provision of essential specifications and feedback will be critical to the networking arrangement. Efficient communication must be a top priority.

Conclusion

What must be done – starting *now*:

1. Catch the vision: we can and will be the BEST!
2. Set our whole organisation on fire with the vision of being the providers of the best quality solutions to our customers (internal, external, existing and potential). There is no textbook approach that will work in every organisation: those who are genuine about achieving superiority will have to take the time and effort to organise themselves and be creative in developing a TQM programme.

3. Have everybody draw up a network of customer-supplier relationships. Once this is done, 'customers' will meet with 'suppliers' and establish target improvements. These should then be integrated into organisation-wide charts, showing not only the relationships but also the goods and services being received and the criteria for measuring quality.
4. Allow full participation; empower and encourage managers and workers to create improvements (no matter how small) in their own tasks. Remember: measurable goals and deadlines must be set to motivate achievement.
5. With full top-management commitment, set up Quality Steering Committees to turbocharge larger quality improvement projects.
6. Set up a suggestion scheme and provide incentives. Stimulate creativity and learning.
7. Train, equip, and motivate everybody to become the best at whatever they are doing – as individuals and as members of their teams.
8. Monitor and sustain *kaizen*: constant improvement involving everyone.
9. Thoroughly investigate how technology can improve quality.
10. Extend the TQM implementation to include customers and suppliers, thus extending the Quality Chain and reducing external weak links that can frustrate internal efforts.
11. Never forget that while we may be the best today, there is never a guarantee that we will still be the best tomorrow. Resting on past or present successes, and becoming complacent, is an epidemic that has been responsible for the fall of nations.

Competitive ferocity is rising sharply. Customer loyalty is decreasing. We can only keep our customers by constantly making sure that we are the best **in their eyes**.

5

THE POWER TRIAD

Preaching to the converted is simple. There is no challenge in convincing those who are already convinced that Quality must be a top priority. Yet how does one convince those who see their jobs merely as a daily routine to keep starvation at bay?

We need to look at the practicalities, issues, and problems from *their* point of view.

Cynicism and resistance to change is to be expected, especially where Quality programmes have been attempted before but have been abandoned because of failure or lack of support, or where things have always been done in a certain way and people see no reason for change. Indeed, people will always resist change if they feel that the change, or the process of achieving the change, is something that they cannot succeed at; will be exceedingly demanding and threatening to their security; or simply unrewarding.

Therefore, when persuading people to put Quality first, one must show that it:

- can be done (with the support they will be given);
- will not threaten;
- will be rewarding – not least of all by securing their jobs and improving opportunities through securing the future success of the organisation.

Slogans like, 'If the team wins – I win!' amount to mere platitudes if managers do not demonstrate, by their systematic and practical support, their genuine commitment.

As in war, rewards must be given. These rewards may be either material or intrinsic – or a combination of both. To develop a desire for victory, allow the soldiers to partake of the spoils. As *The Art of War* puts it:

> *When you plunder the countryside, let the spoil be divided among your men; when you capture new territory, cut it up into allotments for your soldiery.*

Remember: we get more of the behaviour we reward.

In developing a reward system, it is, therefore, first necessary to address the question: what behaviour do we want? We need to consider not only short-term needs, but also long-term and intrinsic needs, such as loyalty and fate sharing.

In addition, a successful solution must:

- be participatively developed;
- focus on the needs of the users, not only on the bottom line;
- be flexible – any system is alive only by virtue of its dependence on humans, thus it must allow for evolution and change.

The Fixed Pie Myth

One of the biggest lies which has robbed organisations of

AS IN WAR, REWARDS MUST BE GIVEN.

their effectiveness, team spirit, and synergy is the Fixed Pie myth. The logic behind this myth lies in the Zero-Sum assumption. The Zero-Sum concept implies that resources and rewards are fixed. Thus, if one party gets an additional X% of the pie, the other will have to lose by the same amount.

The popular support given to the above principle is due to an absence of synergy and an excessive devotion to immediate returns (short-termism mixed with impatience). Synergy takes time to develop. Early on in the learning curve, organisations or projects may suffer low returns. However, with intelligent persistence, the results will exceed the sum of the inputs. The resulting productivity is the proof of synergy.

With synergy and growth, the pie is not fixed but will grow. On the other hand, without these success factors, the pie will shrink and may disappear altogether.

Keys to the Power Triad

This is why the **Quality-Productivity-Motivation Triad** will work:

1. Quality leads to higher prices – people are willing to pay more for a better solution!
2. Quality leads to higher cost-efficiency, including improved stock turnover and lower stocks, reduced wastage, faster delivery and cash flow, and reduction of sales effort required due to natural repurchase.
3. Quality brings about enhanced productivity as a result of eliminating quality control, inspection, and repairs – which, in the longer term, effectively reward poor quality.
4. When combined with higher sales prices and improved cost efficiency, improved productivity means higher profits and cash flows from operations. These gains

will enable greater incentives to be given and more resources to be invested in TQM – which, in turn, will sustain or even accelerate innovation and improvement.

5. As causes for customer dissatisfaction are replaced by improved value and satisfaction, customer loyalty grows.
6. Quality stimulates and raises morale and pride of belonging.
7. Increased application of revenue sharing provides further incentive to expand the revenue pie.
8. Responsibility for own costs by individual divisions and departments motivates better cost control.
9. Bureaucracy and central control will decline. Pyramids will be broken down into networks of 'pancake' organisations. Decisions which relate principally to a specific organisational unit, should insofar as possible, be made by the people in that unit. This, in particular, applies to the way in which the pie is shared – and the way the *slices* are then further divided among members at the *sub-team* level.

The practice suggested, which can be applied partially (especially at the beginning) as a component of total remuneration is as follows:

- Cost centres are made responsible for their own costs, although they should be allowed to borrow from the company.
- Revenue from individual sales is distributed to internal sub-teams, by negotiated agreement among these partners, from the residue of the sales receipts. (The residue being sales receipts less essential provisions for external payments and re-investment.)
- Division within sub-teams to individual members will be again by negotiated agreement among the individuals concerned. This removes bureaucratic control, motivates by empowerment and reduces

75

friction between sub-teams and top management – because bosses can no longer be blamed for bad decisions made by the team.

The practice of divisionalisation and decentralisation should not be taken to the extreme. Beyond a certain point, overall profitability can suffer. This often happens where internal prices are higher than prices from external suppliers, and internal customers buy in from outside. Internal prices are usually developed using a cost-plus method, and thus include an element of fixed cost. Where one department decides to buy in from an external supplier on the basis of price alone, overall profitability may suffer.

Example:

Department A is a supplier to Department B. Department B is able to buy in the same product from an external supplier at £18.50. Department A charges a transfer price of £20, made up as follows:

Department A per-unit price	£
Materials	8
Labour (piecemeal payment)	4
Departmental overhead – variable	2
– fixed	2
(apportioned)	
Head Office overhead (fixed)	2
Total Cost	18
Mark up	2
Transfer Price	20

Assuming that the annual volume that Department B needs of the product is 50,000 units, the overall loss to the company, should Department B purchase these externally, will be:

	£	£
Unit profit contribution **(A's product)**		
Selling price		20
Less avoidable costs:		
– Materials	8	
– Labour	4	
– Variable Overheads	2	
	—	
		(14)
Contribution per unit of sales		6
Savings per unit (to B) from purchasing externally = £20 – £18.50		1.50
Therefore net loss of contribution resulting from external purchase (per unit) = £6 – £1.50		4.50
Loss of profits to the company as a whole = £4.50 × 50,000		£225,000

Even though Department A saves £75,000 by purchasing the product from the external supplier, the company stands to lose £225,000 of profits. Other costs, such as redundancies, may be involved. Strategic disadvantages such as increasing the company's dependence on external suppliers, and loss of control over quality and delivery, are other considerations which have to be taken into account.

In the longer term, however, it can be argued that the fair competition introduced will help identify areas of weakness and lack of competitive ability, so that special management attention can be given to exploit TQM.

A Mathematical Case for the Power Triad

Per Unit	Note	Mediocre Ltd Product X £	High Quality Ltd Product Z £
Selling Price	a	18	21
Costs:			
Material	b	5	6
Labour	c	5	4.5
Overheads – variable	d	2	1.5
– fixed		2	2
		—	—
PROFIT		4	7

Profit per labour hour			
– Product X (2 hrs)		£2.00	
– Product Z (1.5 hrs)			£4.67
Relative productivity			
– Product X (Basis)		1	
– Product Z (4.67/2)			2.33

Notes:

a As product Z is consistently superior to X, it has managed to penetrate better retailers and to achieve a better price.

b The material used in producing X is cheaper (£2.30 per kg), but 8% of the material cost represents wastage. The material for Z is better quality, consequently higher priced at £3 per kg, but there is zero wastage.

c Labour is paid at the rate of £2.50 per hour for X, and £3 per hour for Z. Besides using better quality material and technology, the workers are better skilled at High Quality Ltd and consequently only 1.5 hrs is needed to produce one unit of product Z (as opposed to 2 hours at Mediocre Ltd for product X).

d With higher productivity and faster rate of output, the variable overhead rate at High Quality Ltd is lower than at Mediocre Ltd.

In manufacturing product Z, High Quality Ltd is 133% (i.e. $[2.33 - 1] \times 100\%$) **more** effective than Mediocre Ltd is at manufacturing product X.

The above demonstrates the compounding and leveraging effect of the synergy that can be attained through TQM. Even though the price of product Z is only (slightly less than) 17% more than product X, the profit is higher by 75%. However, the main thing to note is that High Quality Ltd is 133% more productive than Mediocre Ltd.

Not only are the workers at High Quality Ltd likely to be paid more, but their jobs are also likely to be more secure. The reason for this, is clearly that as productivity is a key to competitive ability, High Quality Ltd is likely to be able to survive and excel in the market place, far better than Mediocre Ltd – especially in recessionary times.

6

LEADING AND MANAGING

What is a leader?

A leader is one who forges his people into a team. By example, he begins the transformation of a group of individuals, into a team. He is able to inspire his people to act positively to attain a common goal, moving together as a single body.

A leader sets standards for himself that are beyond the ability of common man. He patterns the standards expected of his team members, but is patient as they develop to attain those standards. By demonstrating self-discipline and humanity, he is able to hold his team together – especially when difficulties strike!

A leader's role is to get the best from his people, in order that he may get the best for them.

From the day he assumes his role, the true leader begins to prepare his team for continuity without him. He understands that he has to make himself expendable. To do this he must not give his people fish – rather, he must teach them to fish for themselves, **as a team**. *Synergy is the phenomenon that* *distinguishes a team from a rabble.*

By instructing, showing, correcting, and guiding, he ensures that on his departure, others within the team will be able to take over his role – and do it well.

Where there is rot in the organisation that cannot be cured, the leader must be willing and able to make painful decisions to remove the sources of the disease. He must be decisive in his action, lest the disease spreads and contaminates the rest of the organisation. Too many otherwise superb managers, because of personal weaknesses, are unable to bring themselves to remove incorrigible weak links; as a result, organisational development is held back unnecessarily and major opportunities lost.

Arguably, even a legend like Chrysler's Lee Iaccoca appears to have failed to achieve the degree of success that might be expected, in providing for a smooth transition in top leadership.

Great leaders never:

- stifle the personal development of their team members;
- take credit for what belongs to the team or a member of the team.

A great American baseball coach is famous for living his philosophy, which goes:

If something goes badly, I did it,
if something goes well, we did it,
if something goes really well, you did it.

Which is the best leadership style?

This is an often asked question, especially by inexperienced managers.

81

The simple answer is: there is no single best leadership (or management) style.

Let's consider the underlying logic for the above statement. No two individuals are alike. And leaders lead people. People may have different attitudes, strengths, weaknesses and be at different stages of development and seniority. Leaders should be consistent – but it would be terribly inconsistent (plus unfair and foolish) to treat different people in the same manner.

As the Americans say, the good leader should use 'different strokes for different folks'. Good leaders should be 'situational': they should adopt styles which suit and are appropriate to the situation and the persons they are dealing with.

The best leaders are thus 'situational leaders' who are competent at using different styles of leadership and management, ranging from instructional through to delegative, according to the stage of development (in a particular role) the person being led is at.

Situational leaders invariably make very flexible leaders – and are adept at catalysing the development of flexible organisations!

Notwithstanding the above, all leaders should:

- lead by consistent example. After all, leaders cannot expect their people to behave better than they do themselves. This would be blatant hypocrisy. And hypocrisy will, sooner or later (but with people getting smarter and smarter, it will probably be sooner) be picked up by those we work with.
- avoid autocracy!
- train and empower those below, then let them get on with their work!

The great leader will possess:

- vision;
- discipline, dedication, and consistency;
- understanding of people in general, but his own people in particular;
- care, respect and a genuine concern for the welfare and prosperity of his team;
- a desire for unity;
- loyalty and self-sacrifice;
- patience;
- ability;
- boldness and courage.

Result: Trust and respect for the leader which leads to robust and effectual teams.

The Five Constants

A leader, being a person ultimately responsible for his team's survival and welfare, must be conversant with five key factors which together determine victory or defeat. Sun Tzu refers to these as the Five Constants, which are:

1. Moral Law

For the successful government of a country, an army, a company, a family, or oneself, there must be a strong sense of purpose, a power which holds the team (or oneself) as one body dedicated to achieving a common goal. Without such a uniting and motivating force, no success can be sustained.

The importance of a uniting sense of purpose is evident in war. In *The Art of War*, it is written:

> *He will win, whose army is animated by the same spirit* ***throughout all*** *its ranks.*

The impact of a change of vision, which is the core of the

HE WILL WIN WHOSE ARMY IS ANIMATED BY THE SAME SPIRIT THROUGHOUT ALL ITS RANKS.

Moral Law, can often be seen when leadership changes hands. New leaders may come in with greater technical expertise, but if they lack the vision, honour, and integrity to inspire loyalty and commitment, and to set the right strategic direction for the organisation, decline will come about before long.

2. Heaven

Heaven stands for the external environmental factors that are beyond the control of mortals. In business this relates to natural developments and macro factors such as international politics, which cannot be directly governed by any individual firm.

3. Earth

Earth is the terrain in which we conduct our warfare. To the military commander, it is the position of the hills, marshlands, clear waters, and narrow passes. To the business strategist, terrain includes the location of target customers, threats of substitutes, local tax laws, industry barriers to entry, supply of skilled labour, and availability of finance.

Terrain factors can sometimes be directly influenced by individual firms. In any event, the strategist must seek ways to manoeuvre around them and, where possible, exploit the opportunities availed.

4. The Commander

The Commander is the strategic spearhead of any operation.

The Commander represents the leadership. In an organisation, the top management make up the Commander. Ultimately the power of the commander is given to him from below. Regardless of the legal authority vested in him, he must have the virtues which will ensure the continued loyalty and commitment of those he oversees. Dictators rule by terror and consequently are never secure from their own people.

The authority of a leader, thus, stems from his qualifications and virtues. To be an inspirational leader, a person must have cultivated self-discipline and consistency, wisdom and competence, empathy and consideration, courage, and honesty. For other desirable attributes, refer to the list at the beginning of this section.

5. Method and Discipline

Even though the Commander may provide the most inspirational leadership possible, and there is great enthusiasm among the workforce, the success will not be sustained if there is no effective system.

Inspiration and enthusiasm, like energy, can be dangerously counterproductive if not properly harnessed and utilised.

To achieve its mission, an organisation must be structured and sub-divided accordingly: each part or function must understand, and be effective in coordinating with the rest. Both management and workers must know their roles and the standard expected from them. Training and equipping must be a top priority. Systems must be used and maintained.

Weak links are eliminated through training, delegating, and communicating.

Developing a Win-Win Organisation

> Organisations, to succeed, must be teams.
> Teams are made up of people.
> People do not naturally work together well.
> Teams do not just happen – they are formed.

The above truisms are obvious – so obvious and logical that

TRAINING AND EQUIPPING MUST BE A TOP PRIORITY.

few organisations seriously address the problem of developing individuals who will make good team members.

People give many reasons why team spirit and commitment are absent from their workplaces. The truth is often hard to accept: leadership is missing.

Great leaders realise that people want to feel great – about themselves and also about others. (How can we really do our best for others if we don't feel good about them?).

This is a radical departure from the normal organisational mentality that says: in order for me to win, someone else has to lose. The radically enlightened, on the contrary, have discovered that sharing the spoils of victory with the team is a powerful way of achieving maximum personal benefits in the long run. That is, of course, nonsense to those trapped by short-termism.

The above Win-Win philosophy is not an airy-fairy ideology that has no empirical basis. Ask the people at Enterprise Oil, which is one of the best companies in Britain (highest productivity, highest pay levels, and lowest labour turnover); they will tell you that the Win-Win philosophy actually works – and amazingly well!

So, a Win-Win environment is needed. This environment can only come about by having lots of Win-Win people.

The leadership approach to cultivating the Win-Win mentality and corporate culture begins with an understanding of the SOBC model:

$$S \longrightarrow O \longrightarrow B \longleftrightarrow C$$

1. External stimuli (S), good or bad, are received by the organism (O, i.e. the human being in this context).

2. The organism responds to the stimuli; this response is termed the behaviour (B).
3. The behaviour gives rise to a consequence (C).
4. The consequence either reinforces or alters the behaviour; i.e. the next time the same stimulus is received, owing to the lessons learned by virtue of the consequence of the previous experience, the organism will either react in the same way – if the consequence the last time was 'good' – or differently – if the consequence was 'bad'.

We should note, however, that because there is a strong interaction between behaviour and consequence, the consequence may end up being a self-perpetuating behaviour. This can be a great thing if the behaviour is positive and favourable but, if not, it can be very counter-productive.

Take greed, for example. Greed stimulates behaviour that is solely motivated to satiating self-gratification and gain. But as greed, like a cancer, is seldom satiable, behaviour that is directed solely to this end will only give rise to greater greed, which then results in even more feverish attempts to gain more . . . and so it continues in a vicious, self-feeding, self-perpetuating cycle that may come to an end only with the demise of the organism.

The behavioural principle described above is referred to as the SOBC (Stimulus-Organism-Behaviour-Consequence) model, and is the basis of many of the great teaching and learning methods (such as operant conditioning).

Simply put, the principle is that behaviour can be shaped (through the learning process) by the use of stimuli and consequence.

To illustrate the implications of this model for leaders and managers let us consider the following passage:

89

Children Learn What They Live

If a child lives with criticism, he learns to condemn,
If a child lives with hostility, he learns to fight,
If a child lives with ridicule, he learns to be shy,
If a child lives with shame, he learns to feel guilty,
If a child lives with tolerance, he learns to be patient,
If a child lives with encouragement, he learns confidence,
If a child lives with praise, he learns to appreciate,
If a child lives with fairness, he learns justice,
If a child lives with security, he learns to have faith,
If a child lives with approval, he learns to like himself,
If a child lives with acceptance and friendship,
. . . . . . he learns to find love in the world.

Although the above passage is self-explanatory, let us use the SOBC model to structure the message it contains, remembering that in a very real way, we are all children with much to learn.

Stimulus	Behaviour/Consequence
NEGATIVE:	
Criticism	Condemns
Hostility	Aggression
Ridicule	Low self-esteem
Shame	Guilt

The ultimate consequence is that the organism (person) cannot receive and appreciate the goodness and potential in themselves and other people. This means that sustained, prosperous teamwork will not happen.

Positive stimuli, on the other hand, release the power within individuals to come together with others to achieve true, organisation-transforming synergy!

90

Stimulus	Behaviour/Consequence
POSITIVE:	
Tolerance	Patience
Encouragement	Self-esteem
Praise	Appreciation
Fairness	Just behaviour
Security	Trust
Approval	Self-acceptance
Acceptance and friendship	Love

On this note, let us direct our attention to the functional activities of management.

What is a Manager?

He is one who gets things done through others; he is a *delegator*.

His traditional role, according to management thinkers like Henry Fayol and F W Taylor, comprised the following functions:

- planning;
- organising;
- communicating;
- directing;
- coordinating.

For leaders, a revised perspective of a manager's role is: to get the best from and for his people.

Remember: People perform well when they feel good, but they perform best when they feel best.

The underlying aim should be not only to develop individuals, but to achieve sustainable and constantly

91

improving synergy. Synergy happens when the product exceeds the sum of the parts:

$$1 + 1 + 1 = 5!$$

The clever combatant looks to the effect of combined energy and does not require too much from individuals. He takes individual talent into account, and uses each man according to his capabilities. He does not demand perfection from the untalented.

Sun Tzu.

Thus, synergy results not only in superior outcomes, but also in reducing the impact of individual weaknesses. Those who are weak in a certain area, will have their weakness neutralised by another who is strong in that same area.

Managers must thus systematically develop their knowledge of their own people so that they may be utilised best.

Management approaches to avoid

Adopting monkeys
This means not doing the work of our team members for them – i.e. letting them deal with their own 'monkeys' (so that they will learn) – don't adopt them!

The Seagull manager
A seagull manager:

flies in,
   makes a lot of noise,
      drops 'puddles' on everyone,
         then flies off.

'Seagulls' do not add value to the team – just aggravation.

The invisible manager

This manager:

- is never there when you need him,
- has little time for you,
- provides little by way of constructive feedback,
- does not reply to memos and reports which he asks for,
- walks past as if you were the invisible one.

In short, it would be better for everyone else on the team if they actually vanished!

The Magpie manager
A magpie is a thief.

Certainly, one of the worst things a manager can do to his subordinates is to steal from them. Years ago, as a young consultant with a major consultancy, I took the initiative of writing a proposal which I felt would greatly enhance the company's professionalism and speed. Obviously, my superior felt the same way – for he sent the proposal under his own name to the chairman, who was delighted by it. Any respect I had for my manager vanished when I discovered what he did.

Instead of stealing, we should be giving credit. Besides this being the ethical thing to do, the resulting dividends in terms of loyalty, comradeship, and commitment from those we manage will be rich indeed.

The Ostrich manager
The proverbial ostrich hides its head in the sand to avoid seeing imminent dangers. Its philosophy is: what I cannot see, cannot harm me.

No matter how tightly we close our eyes, if a three-ton truck is hurtling straight towards us, that is a reality which is going to badly affect us, unless we move out of the way.

Instead of soaring like hawks, 'ostriches' miss opportunities and are unable to avoid crises because they are caught in the activity trap. Activity traps are often of their own creation because of their failure to delegate.

Ostrich managers also practise the height of irresponsibility as through their actions, they often make victims out of their people.

*(Refer to Appendix I (page 161) for The Chicken manager)

Six key responsibilities

We must aim to get these areas right to get the best from and for our people.

1. Recruitment

The aim of recruitment is to add strength to the organisational body, not to introduce cancers!

Look not only for requisite talent or skills, but also probe to ensure that culture, attitude, character, and personality are, or have the potential to be, compatible with our organisational culture.

The charismatic president of the Elim Pentecostal movement in the UK, Rev Wynne Lewis, described how he selects job applicants. 'I take them for a walk around the grounds [where there is invariably litter]. If they are spontaneous in picking up the litter, then I know that they probably have the right attitude – and the initiative – we want in our people.'

The lesson here is: hire people with initiative – those who will not wait for others to do what should be done. They must be willing to dirty their hands and do tasks which *prima donnas* might consider demeaning. Avoid those who esteem themselves too highly for they cannot be relied upon in times of need.

It must be clearly recognised that it is necessary to invest time, money and effort to ensure that the people we accept have the ability to be truly great players in our team.

In recruiting, it is also important to remember that we must not misrepresent prospects. In this way, dreams are cruelly shattered and disaffection from within, cultivated.

The cost of hiring the wrong people can be horrendous: organisational disruption; sabotage; worsening industrial relations leading to strikes; impact on morale; waste of management time in dealing with these problems; recruitment costs; training replacements; dismissal payoffs; and potentially the worst of all: breeding the most dangerous enemy, *the enemy from within.*

2. Induction

All new recruits or those newly transferred within the organisation should be inducted properly; do not assume that they are comfortable without this or already know enough and will soon learn the ropes on their own. Such an attitude stems from a lack of care and consideration.

We need to ensure that we have adequately prepared the new member to become part of the team by asking:

- Have we made their roles and responsibilities absolutely clear to them?
- Do they know the standard expected (in quantifiable terms)?
- Have we (participatively) set goals for them to work to?

Note: Uncertainty arising from poor induction and inadequate (or zero) feedback can be very unhealthy, especially for those lacking in self-confidence.

Participative goal-setting is necessary on an on-going basis if systematic and constant improvement is to be achieved.

Goals, to be effective, must be:

- challenging;
- achievable;
- measurable (this must be supported by a recording or accounting system of accepted accuracy and integrity);
- rewarding – if they are achieved.

3. Equipment
A good manager is consistently just and fair. It would be unfair to expect a person to do a job for which he is not properly equipped, i.e. if he does not have the right working environment, team support or necessary tools.

Provide for the needs of your people and they will provide for the needs of your customers.

4. Education and Training
We have already looked at training in the context of Total Quality Management. Now let us elaborate further.

Education focuses on developing the person, training focuses on the skills. To get the synergy we need to be dynamically competitive, education and training programmes should be oriented towards team development, not only within the natural group (e.g. department) but also between different parts of the organisation.

Having recruited people with development potential, it is important not just to develop their skills. Cultural development and bonding are important needs which must not be neglected.

The best technical training in the world will be wasted and may even be counterproductive if the *person* is not developed so as to be motivated to use, and share, his skills for the benefit of the team. Highly-developed skills in the wrong hands can be lethal.

The goal of training is not just efficiency and effectiveness. These are, of course, important results. However, ability to work without supervision should also be clearly prioritised. Successful training should produce individuals who are competently independent, yet good teamworkers. Consequently, unnecessary hand-holding, duplication and overlaps are reduced or eliminated.

Individual competence within an effectively coordinated team frees managers to concentrate on the functions of management: analysis, planning, coordinating, organising, directing, and leading.

A wealth of empirical evidence exists which demonstrates that businesses, like Richard Branson's Virgin, which grow organically (through training and promotion of people from within) tend to out-perform those which grow inorganically (by recruiting outsiders for senior posts).

The reason for the difference in outcome is not difficult to understand. Look at the Japanese. Their firms have traditionally provided lifetime job security and recognition for seniority. As a result, enhanced morale and trust result.

Trust and integrity, as with loyalty, develop by first flowing downwards: i.e. yet again, it begins with top management.

5. Encouragement
To reinforce positive behaviour, we should remember to praise (but not flatter) the behaviour and the person. It is rewarding for both the giver and the recipient.

A useful tip is that giving public recognition to someone in their absence can be motivational for both the person being praised as well as those present. Good news will often reach the ears of the 'praisee'. Often praising when the person concerned is not present works better than when the former is present as the latter can lead to embarrassment or suspicion that an ulterior motive is involved.

In delivering public recognition, care needs to be taken. If not, resentment instead of encouragement may result. Negative outcomes may arise when those present feel threatened by the enhanced prestige given to someone who may be, in their eyes, a rival. Additionally, the person being praised may let the praise 'go to his head', and become arrogant and obnoxious.

It is thus important to praise the specific behaviour but not belittle others by comparison, or overdo the praise.

Note: Others also need encouragement. Often encouragement is most needed by people who have made mistakes, failed or are frustrated.

As managers we should never forget that we are managing people and not robots. Unlike machines, people respond to respect and sincerity.

The authors of the best-seller *The One Minute Manager* argue that when mistakes occur, true encouragement does not say, 'That's all right. Forget about it. It could happen to anyone.' Upon finding out all the facts, a swift reprimand might be the right thing to do. If this is the case, then what should be said may be along the following lines:

> *That was a mistake. The reasons why things turned out the way they did were . . . I am upset with the outcome and I do not want this mistake to recur. However, I know you better than that. This behaviour was unlike you.*

Don't let the team/us down again in this way. I know that you are capable of much better work.

Note that the final praise element is focused on the person and not his negative behaviour.

Practical point: Unlike praise, a reprimand should be made in private and, if feasible, remain confidential. This avoids humiliation and helps develop trust. 'Loss of face' (the oriental expression for humiliation) breeds resentment and blocks learning, thus producing negative consequences.

To maximise effectiveness, both praise and reprimands should be delivered *as soon as possible* after the event. To heighten the effectiveness and sustained impact of praise, a touch on the shoulder or the elbow, may be used. Beware, however, as this 'bonding' should only be used if trust has been established satisfactorily between the parties.

What about punishment?

Firstly, we need to clarify what we mean by punishment. Intention, perception and result are factors which need to be considered.

Responses to misdemeanour or poor performance, such as dismissal, demotion, and reduction in pay, are commonly considered to be punishment. The argument offered in support of such practices is that they are used to enforce discipline, and to fail to do so would invite the perception that *management's kindness is weakness*: dangerous precedents would erode morale by eroding discipline and authority.

Discipline and authority are vital. There is no disputing that. However, while reprimand is an important management tool, an even more powerful approach is stimulating respect and discipline by example.

My view is that it is unrealistic and naive to believe that there is no place in the world for punishment. I am grateful to my parents and teachers who punished me for the right reasons, i.e. *for my benefit*. This, I believe is the key. Punishment should be carried out for constructive reasons: to change attitudes and behaviour. Punishment should never be delivered out of anger or impulse, but only in accordance with rules which have been clearly communicated to the person at fault *prior* to his offence. The system of rewards and consequences must be fair and understood by all. Care and concern must underlie the punishment and, to exact maximum effect, let these positive motives be perceived by the recipient of the punishment. The fault must be proven to be attributable to the person who is to be punished. Genuine ignorance, resulting from the failure of the establishment to communicate effectively the expected standard, and consequences of failure, is and should be accepted as an extenuating factor.

To be effective, punishment must be *seen to be fair*. This means that a clear explanation must be given – and that the defaulter accepts the punishment. Acceptance of the expected performance standards and the consequences of deviation (reward as well as reprimand or punishment) must be achieved for the system to be seen to be fair. Achieving a perception of fairness is important for morale. Humiliation should be avoided if at all possible. Unless the person receiving the punishment is to be removed from the organisation, he should be assisted in being re-admitted to the fold. Once a mistake has been dealt with, it should not be referred to again. But the lesson should be retained, otherwise the corrective action taken will have been in vain.

It is usually better to err on the side of mercy. There will be situations when circumstances dictate severe action. A situation could exist where retaining an errant employee would pose a serious threat to the organisation, but often a reprimand, if well delivered, can be the most effective punishment.

There will always be situations when punishment will be necessary, and even desirable. Notwithstanding, inspiration, encouragement, and motivation should be used instead.

Unless accepted as being fair, the person to be punished will view the punishment as being directed at him personally and not at his behaviour. Consequently, he focuses not on his negative behaviour, but on the punisher. Where this is the case, resentment and bitterness will be likely to develop.

Punishment is therefore most effective when a firm bond of mutual respect exists between the person meting out the punishment (the superior) and the person receiving it. The relationship makes it obvious that the act is being taken without malice, but rather with respect and at a personal cost to the superior.

A system that includes punishments must be more than balanced by positive rewards. Otherwise morale will not improve.

Leaders and managers would therefore be well advised to cultivate a strong bond of trust and mutual respect with their team members.

As Sun Tzu remarks:

> If soldiers are punished before they have grown attached to you, they will not prove obedient; and unless obedient, they will be practically useless. If, when soldiers have become attached to you, punishments are not enforced, they will still be useless. Therefore, soldiers must be treated in the first instance with humanity, but kept under control by means of iron discipline. This is a certain road to victory.

While the strict practice of Sun Tzu's advice may not be advisable in many modern organisations (perhaps except for the armed forces and penal institutions) the core principles are:

- build the bond;
- be consistent – if the system is good, apply it.

In the final analysis, what is important is learning, which results in attitudinal and behavioural change. Only then can the recurrence of mistakes be avoided.

Deviating slightly, if anyone truthfully believes that he has never made a mistake, it is likely that he has in fact made the biggest one: failure to experiment and innovate. So, if we have not been making any mistakes lately, let us ask ourselves: have we been trying hard enough to improve?

To achieve constant improvement, leading to becoming 'the very best', one must be prepared to try new and radical things.

> *One with knowledge but without courage is like a dog that can only bark.*
>
> Chinese proverb.

6. Motivation

The process of motivation, like customer research, begins by finding out what will stimulate and sustain positive behaviour.

Through a package made up of performance-related remuneration, promotion, training, encouragement and delegation, management must accommodate the fundamental needs of the workforce.

Allowing and encouraging self-actualisation through the decentralisation of monolithic bureaucracies into small, flatly-organised teams – adequately equipped and trained – will generate team pride and spirit which will meet both social and status needs. A further benefit is that teams and their members will be more directly able to see the impact of their work on the success of the team. This contributes to self-actualisation: the highest need and motivator.

An approach which exemplified the above principles was developed at Volvo. The core bases of the Volvo Team system were:

- autonomous teams,
- self recording of performance,
- job rotation to eliminate weak links within the team.

This has been adapted and adopted successfully by organisations all over the world. It is a practical application of the specialisation and decentralisation methods advocated above.

The Five Fatal Mistakes

Sun Tzu wrote that there are five mistakes that a general or leader can make that may result in destruction by the enemy. This is still true today.

The five mistakes are:

1. Cowardice
A coward dies many times, so the saying goes. One who lacks the backbone and strength to realise his convictions will never achieve much. Not only will he not dare to try the things that may result in great advances, but he will never gain the respect and loyalty of those who have to work with him. Cowards may make fewer mistakes because they shun all risk, but ultimately they pay the price for being losers. Their knowledge of vital matters will always be superficial due to their lack of personal experience and achievement.

103

Honour, which is a core pre-requisite of leadership, demands courage.

Cowardice is to be distinguished from discretion. The wise will always assess a situation well before acting. The wisest thing a general can do in a situation where the enemy forces are far superior and where escape is possible is to order a retreat. This is not cowardice; this is wisdom which opposes waste and the foregoing of future victories.

2. Recklessness and impatience

The opposite of cowardice is recklessness. A person who is reckless demonstrates shallowness and incompetence.

Recklessness is acting without thinking and with inadequate preparation. Through this, many have succumbed to traps laid by the enemy.

Do not be persuaded to move when in a position of weakness and unpreparedness. But when you do move, move with lightning speed. As a siege is the worst tactic in battle, there is little to be gained and much to be lost in business by sluggish implementation and fussiness. As the great seventh-century Chinese general Li Ching expounded:

> To the soldier, overwhelming speed is of paramount importance and he must never miss [true] opportunities.

Impatience, however, often leads to regrettable mistakes. It is often advisable to wait for an adequate period before finalising important decisions. While aggression is desirable in a leader, those who are aggressive are also often impulsive. Thus, they make and execute decisions which they may regret soon after.

Time tempers all impulses and soothes all hurt. Thus allow enough time between the making of a decision and communicating or executing it to ensure that it is rational and correct.

3. Excessive concern for the short-term welfare of the people

A leader is a father to his people. But he should be a wise father.

As some parents tend to spoil their children, so some leaders spoil their people by being too concerned about their short-term welfare. Failure to reprimand and exact discipline are examples of this mistake. Excessive protectiveness is another. As industrial protectionism beyond the short term is never a good economic policy, so being excessively protective of the people within any organisation is a bad thing. It robs them of the opportunity to learn, mature, become self-sufficient and capable of fully contributing to the attainment of dynamic synergy within their team.

Protectionism may also work in favour of the competition. Take, for example, the growing lobby in the US to impose more restrictive quotas on Japanese cars. Even though the Japanese image of being unerring may have been tarnished somewhat of late, they are still a force very much to be reckoned with. Knowing their mentality, what may well happen as a result is as follows:

a) Complacency among American car manufacturers and their workforce. 'Buy America' may in the short term persuade consumers to buy American made, regardless of the lower quality and value. Complacency tends to have a tendency to slow down the pace of improvement, or even reverse such a trend.

b) The Japanese, forced into a corner in which they have to fight for their lives, will, in their indomitable style, rise to the challenge. National pride and honour will be at stake. Their response will be to accelerate the rate of improvement and increase value.

c) As the value gap widens in favour of Japanese cars, the American consumers, though wanting to do the right and patriotic thing, will reluctantly but increasingly realise that as their economic troubles deepen with no end in sight, prudence and economic rationality must prevail. Thus, they will again begin to buy, motivated not by patriotic stirrings, but by economic sense. And they will buy Japanese (and Korean, Taiwanese, Malaysian . . .).

So much for global protectionism.

When it comes to organisations, some managers tend to give too much too early. As a consequence, their people view the rewards as being cheap and grow to expect the practice of getting much for little. This makes organisations sluggish, unproductive, and ultimately, ill equipped to survive.

The lesson for leaders is to be disciplined with yourself: over-generosity is a fault. Reward your people by all means, but timing is vital. Share the spoils of victories and successes with the *soldiers* who have actively participated in achieving the victory. Do not reward *passengers*.

Setting precedents that cannot, and should not, be maintained is dangerous. When generosity must come to an end, for example, if resources have been depleted as a result of mismanagement, disenchantment and division will result. Avoid the famine by being prudent with the conduct of feasts.

Prudence and caution are great virtues that help avoid mistakes made through haste. For this reason, do not despise those who advocate caution. Seek to understand their viewpoint, for wisdom is often misperceived as pessimism or lack of courage. A team full of optimists is a dangerous thing. 'Yes-men' are no help in times of difficulty. Opposing perspectives openly discussed will result in better balanced and superior solutions. Blessed is the leader who has a wise counsellor, a devil's advocate, on his team.

In rewarding, seek to motivate people to acquire the characteristics and skills that will add value and strength to the team. Seek to cultivate the group rather than the individual.

Change, especially in culture, is always painful. Expect difficulties, but remain strong in resolve. Do not lower the standard expected as long as it is achievable. Standards are of no use if they do not challenge and create new thresholds of endurance. Set a high standard and demonstrate uncompromising commitment to it. Through wise management, cause every member of the team to rise to the standard set.

Lowering standards just because the team members are experiencing discomfort is a sign of weakness and myopia. Learning pains are inevitable and desirable for toughening and refining. The higher the price, the more precious the prize.

Leaders should identify the characteristics of the people they want in their teams, and direct their management focus and reward system to the development of these corporate virtues. Loyalty is a great virtue that is neglected in the West. Cultivate loyalty, so that in difficult times the team will stand together and exploit their adversity.

In times of peace, prepare for war.

4. Arrogance
Beware of arrogance, for it blinds one to hidden dangers, and to learning. A most dangerous expression of arrogance is belittling and underestimating the enemy. Respect potential enemies, no matter how insignificant they presently are, for even great oak trees grow from little acorns.

Respect, also, small customers and allies, for they, too, may grow into powerful and valuable friends. Should one who is great help and treat with respect one who is less significant, their respect and gratitude may one day richly repay the earlier kindness received.

Such behaviour toward those whom others may see as being inconsequential is not only good investment, but desirable for the development of a wholesome and fulfilling culture.

Respect for all without undue discrimination will lead to greater security and strength, and the conversion of enemies into allies.

Unlike the wise, the arrogant are slow to listen, and fast to speak. In such manner is arrogance the father of ignorance, for where one refuses to listen, how can one grow wise? In *Desiderata* is found a profound admonition:

> *Listen to the foolish, for even they have their story.*

Arrogance is the surest path to decline. Thus, be wary of those who flatter; test their sincerity and intentions. Gather around you those who have the courage of conviction, and will, in loyalty, point out failings and weaknesses. These are friends worth cultivating. Honesty is difficult, especially when it concerns faults, but it is the proof of loyalty and friendship.

Those who are arrogant will fail to take adequate precautions. When they make mistakes, they will refuse to acknowledge that they have done so. Often such persons are quick to re-allocate the blame. Sun Tzu advocates:

> *Pretend to be weak, that [your enemy] may grow arrogant.*

Additionally, cultivate a sense of humility, for truly, there will always be a mountain higher than our own.

The more puffed up they are, the heavier they fall.

Arrogance is, however, not to be confused with healthy pride, which is self-esteem. A vision that is being realised will bring about pride. No worthy organisation can sustain itself without the self-esteem that will stimulate boldness and perpetuate progressiveness.

5. Tempestuousness and sensitivity to insults
There would be fewer bullfights if bulls were less tempestuous and easily infuriated.

A frequent cause of tempestuous response is an excessively delicate honour, i.e. ego. In war, an often effective tactic is to infuriate the other party by challenging his honour. In the ring, a skilful fighter will often goad his opponent to anger, causing him to lose composure and control. Sugar Ray Leonard was a master of this tactic. Sun Tzu's advice is:

If your opponent is of a choleric temper, seek to irritate him.

Tempestuousness which results from the enemy's action must not be confused with rousing oneself before battle. The latter is an effective way of increasing and focusing one's energy for the task at hand. As Sun Tzu writes in his chapter on *waging war:*

Now, in order to kill the enemy, our men must be roused to anger.

In martial arts, a method of increasing a fighter's effectiveness is to condition the combatant so that when he is hit, he will automatically convert the pain into anger; the anger into power – and the power into devastation. Thus, through this means, the fighter is able to use the opponent's energy against himself.

In preparing to use this tactic, remember the exhortation from *The Art of War*:

> *Though the enemy be stronger in numbers, we may prevent him from fighting. Scheme to discover his plans and the likelihood of their success. Rouse him, and learn the principle of this activity and inactivity. Force him to reveal himself so as to find out his vulnerable spots.*

In war and business, as far as dealing with the opposition is concerned, use subtlety and deception:

> *If weak, pretend to be strong; if strong pretend to be weak; if near, give the appearance of being far away; if far away, make the enemy believe that you are at his gate.*

So vital a part of practical wisdom is the art of deception that Sun Tzu referred to it in the following manner:

> *O divine art of subtlety and secrecy! Through you we learn to be invisible, through you inaudible, and hence we can hold the enemy's fate in our hands.*

Note well the art and psychology of warfare.

The Six Ways of Courting Defeat

The five fatal mistakes are personal weaknesses of character that should not be evident in a leader. To these, Sun Tzu adds six ways of courting defeat.

1. Neglecting to assess the strength of the opposition

> *If you know the enemy and know yourself, you need not fear the result of a hundred battles. If you know yourself*

but not the enemy, for every victory gained, you will also suffer a defeat. If you know neither the enemy nor yourself, you will succumb in every battle.

Sun Tzu.

Without knowledge of the opposition, how can a leader plan his strategy and provide the resources needed to implement the plan? If an enemy is far superior in every way, then a head-on confrontation may be most unwise and unhealthy. If an enemy is equally matched in resources, we must plan to deplete his resources by appropriating them for our own use:

For every ton of our enemy's grain that we so appropriate for ourself, its benefit to us will be as twenty tons of our own grain.

We are reminded again of the importance of gathering and using information to achieve and secure our competitive advantages.

We need to work out how the opposition will try to exploit opportunities in the market place, even as we will, to gain the upper hand. The strategic leader will then devise strategies and counter-strategies to neutralise or even gain an advantage from the opposition's actions. Benefiting from the competition's activities, and keeping the latter ignorant of our advantage, is a true mark of excellence. This should be the champion's aim.

As long as the information is true and relevant, each hour spent studying it will save several hours of ineffective action and unnecessary wastage of resources. This is wisdom.

2. Lack of Authority
This stems from one of the five fatal mistakes: the personal trait of cowardice. Assertiveness – not autocracy – is a vital leadership characteristic.

Even though all leaders should encourage active participation (to the extent that is commensurate with the ability of the individual concerned), leaders should lead by *consensus*, not by *permission*. Consensus means receiving ideas and being open to desirable change. Ultimately, however, the leader has to make the decision and accept the responsibility for the consequences.

Lack of authority implies a lack of backbone and conviction. This is damaging to discipline and morale.

Relevant to our discussion is the issue of how much should one divulge to subordinates. On less sensitive issues, full disclosure may be appropriate. On matters that are confidential or sensitive, caution is necessary. Until someone has been faithful over a sustained period of time, do not be too trusting, for injury may befall not only yourself but others who depend upon you. Remember that sensitive information is a weapon that can cause great destruction if wielded by the wrong person.

3. Defective Training

As I have stressed, good training is vital. Champions get to where they are by doing more high-quality training than others.

Effective training is a matter of both:

- quality – in terms of relevance and impact;
- quantity – frequency is necessary for reinforcement, continuity, and progress.

Part of any organisation's strategic review (which should be carried out by top management every six to twelve months) should be a training needs and performance analysis. This will help determine the effectiveness of the training. Together with an assessment of strategic needs, highly-focused training programmes should be developed.

4. Unjustifiable Anger

Unjustifiable anger causes one to lose the ability to think and act rationally. Timing will be sacrificed as actions are executed prematurely. Irrational actions will result in painful and regrettable outcomes. With leaders, such behaviour will not just hurt themselves, but also the people they are meant to be leading.

The lack of self-control is also a very poor example to set: such behaviour should be discouraged rather than propagated.

Those who are naturally tempestuous and prone to loss of temper must recognise that this is a serious shortcoming. Patience and self-control must be cultivated without compromise.

5. Disregard of Discipline

While unnecessary rules and all forms of dysfunctional bureaucracy should be avoided, discipline should never be compromised. Discipline is the foundation of morale and order.

Where a leader flouts the standard and behavioural norms that have been set, the system and efficiency of his organisation, and consequently its ability and reputation, will suffer.

Leaders must personify discipline and all the other attributes which are expected from members of the organisation. Because of their visibility, they must seek to avoid the mistakes and departures from good behaviour that may be pardonable if committed by another with less responsibility. Consistent avoidance of negative behaviour is almost impossible; this may be the reason why there are so few genuinely worthy 'heroes' around today. Even Paul the Apostle was inspired to write:

For what I do is not the good I want to do; no, the evil I do not want to do – this I keep on doing.

Romans 7:19

A leader, depending on how seriously he takes his mandate and responsibilities, is often in a very lonely position. Leaders must stand above the others. To shine bright as a beacon, they must learn self-control to resist the temptations that would otherwise tarnish their impact.

6. Failure to use individuals according to their strengths

Strengths encompass not only skills and experience, but also personality and character.

Synergy is achieved by building a team in such a way so as to maximise the combined abilities of the individuals in it. For synergy to develop, therefore, the proper composition of teams, and division of duties according to their differing strengths, are vital.

To form an effective organisation or team, it is important to choose motivated persons of potential. The training should be to develop *general* ability as well as to further develop *individual* strengths and specialisms. The end result that we should consciously aim for should, however, be a strong *team*, rather than strong individuals.

Rewards should also be directed at the team more than at individuals. This principle is key to the management practice of developing team consensus before a decision is implemented. An individual may propose an idea, but the idea is passed on to the rest of the team for comments and suggestions with the final approval being the domain of the leader of the team (insofar as the decision concerned is a matter which the team is authorised to implement).

In using individuals according to their strengths, comparative ability, as against absolute superiority, must be taken into account. Depending on the function of the team, and the situation concerned, flexibility in roles is desirable. Rotating jobs within the organisation to gain exposure to other areas and functions may help the performance of staff. They are then likely to be better able to relate to other departments (especially as they will know people from these departments personally), and to see problems and issues from diverse perspectives.

Conclusion

Prosperity comes with training, equipping and dealing correctly with people. Wisdom must make use of the experience of the ages – not least of which is derived from encounters on the battlefield.

Fairness and genuine concern for one's people, while at the same time being very goal-oriented are hallmarks of the good leader/manager. But the wise general knows that excessive rewards and over-generosity can spoil the potential for excellence, unity and loyalty in his people.

The skills of leadership can be learnt and developed, but only with conscientious practice. Patience, discipline, and perseverance are key to leadership success.

By getting the best from your people, you will be getting the best for them.

Remember: *If the customer wins, we (the team) win; if we win, I win.*

The following management principles will help to turn people into champion teams:

- set goals participatively;
- praise positive behaviour;

- reprimand negative behaviour;
- be consistent.

Finally, let us remind ourselves that effectual management begins with the disciplined management of *oneself*.

7

INNOVATIVE MARKETING

There are many sophisticated definitions of the word 'marketing', but, for most of us, simple and practical explanations work better. Marketing is simply the process of:

- finding out what the customer wants;
- providing it, in such a way that we also get what we want.

Many still confuse marketing with 'sales' or 'advertising', or both. However, from the above explanation of what marketing really means, it becomes clear that marketing is not a specialised function at all. There is no mystery to it: it covers, directly or indirectly, the whole process of staying in business.

The Objectives of Marketing

Theodore Leavitt made famous the following truism:

> *Nobody buys a product or service, people buy solutions to their needs.*

117

What the customer wants is, therefore, a situational expression of a need. *Needs* do not change, but the *wants* do. For example, people will always have status needs. In days gone by, this need might have been met by having an elaborate horse-drawn carriage. Today, the same need may be met by having a chauffeured Rolls Royce.

If a need is not met, frustration develops.

Marketing's sole function may, thus, be stated to be: **to differentiate in our favour**. This means that we will take the steps necessary to ensure that our customers see that what we offer meets their needs better than anyone else's product. Consequently, the focus of marketing strategy must be to optimise the positioning of the product (or service or organisation) in the minds of our target customers.

Differentiation that is neither wanted nor appreciated by the customer can not only be a waste of time and money, but it can also result in customer disenchantment. Allow me to illustrate this point. I once passed a curio shop which had a wooden box displayed in its window. The box had a thin layer of veneer over the lid, and on this veneer was a garish painting. The result? It was 'cheap and nasty'. Although I collect wooden boxes, this one was not one I would take home, even if it had been given to me for free!

Consequently, the differentiation of the veneer and the painting, though no doubt involving extra cost, was nonetheless counter-productive (as far as I was concerned)!

Business Orientations

There are various ways of running a business. The different ways reflect the different attitudes or orientations of the organisations concerned.

Let's explore a few of the orientations:

Sales-led

Organisations which are *sales-led* can be identified by their 'hard sell' approach. Essentially, their main focus is to sell their product, without adaptation to the needs of the customer, by using tactics which exert pressure on the customer to buy.

This approach may not be too much of a problem if what is being sold is what the customer wants. But often this is not the case.

In the early days, the 'hard sell' was a very popular approach especially in certain industries, such as insurance and home appliances (vacuum cleaners in particular). It is still very much practised by timeshare salespeople.

Heavy or high-pressure selling has tarnished the reputation of salespeople in general. This is really a shame, as salespeople should be seen as the heroes who keep economies moving, not parasites.

Product-led

Some companies focus on the quality of their products, which is great if their definition of quality happens to coincide with the customer's.

By focusing on their products (and such companies tend to become overly sensitive and arrogant about their products), these companies often treat customers as 'necessary inconveniences' and certainly not the VIPs that they really are.

Customers are seen as of secondary importance to the product, and the attitude of the vendor is that 'we know best' (so don't bother us with your silly questions and impertinent complaints).

Years ago, Amstrad, the computer manufacturer, launched a

new product to compete against IBM's PCs. The Amstrad computer was apparently a superior machine, which, unlike the PC, did not require a cooling fan and an air vent. So, the Amstrad machine was made without the fan and vent, even though customers voiced their concern about the absence of these features.

Alan Sugar, the chairman of Amstrad, admitted later that ignoring his customers contributed to the difficult times which Amstrad would subsequently experience. While Amstrad was, in the main, not a typical product-led company, this event helps to highlight the danger of ignoring one's customers.

There is also a well known story about the 'best mouse-trap in the world'. The story goes that a man came up with an idea for a mouse-trap that would be more effective at catching (and killing) mice than any other mouse-trap available. He was right: his mouse-trap worked better than anything else on the market. Naturally, the entrepreneur was euphorically optimistic. He confidently boasted, 'The world will beat a path to my door.'

Regrettably, the sales and profits he expected never materialised. Why?

You see, the main problem was that he was a man. Users of mouse traps were mainly women (in that part of the world in those days). So, he did not appreciate that his trap, which exterminated rodents so effectively, posed problems as far as the prospective customers were concerned – because the traps were just *too* effective.

The two primary problems were:

- by doing the job, the trap would at the end of the day contain one dead (and slightly mangled) mouse, which had to be extricated manually – the urban lady folk, being somewhat squeamish, did not relish this task;

- mice may constitute a nuisance, but they have soft fur, rounded ears and (to some) cute faces: consequently, ladies felt guilty about *murdering* them.

It shows again that the customer is not to be ignored, but loved, and understood!

Production-led

Companies in Eastern Europe are still suffering from being production-led: a throw-back to the days when their economies were stringently centrally planned. As such companies were appraised on how well they achieved the centrally planned production targets, which were seldom concerned with quality. They did not have to plan for themselves, and they did not have to sell (the foreign trade companies and the centrally planned purchases by state-owned retailers saw to that). Thus, the manufacturers were purely production units. As such their orientation was, understandably, wholly production-led.

There were other orientations, but perhaps the point has already been well made. So without further ado, we go onto the winning orientation:

Customer-Led, Market-Driven

This orientation is based on the Golden Rule of business:

He who has the gold, makes the rules.

Put another way, the customer is our MIP (Most Important Person), and the reason why we are in business.

Although we need to gather comprehensive knowledge of the market forces, the key focus must remain the customer. The customer is the spearhead and prime focus of our knowledge quest. Getting to know intimately what the ultimate judge and paymaster desires is indeed a worthwhile investment of time and money.

The governing principle which underpins our every action should be that we are here first and foremost to serve the customer – by giving him what he needs. In order to do so, we have to manage ourselves and our resources, in a volatile business environment, very effectively indeed. This approach is more than logical, it is commonsensical.

We can only profit and grow by meeting our customer's needs. In practical terms, we must develop the products/services that will satisfy the customer; charge the right price; place the goods where the customer will buy them; make certain the customer is aware of the existence of what we are offering; and ensure that the customer's awareness is then converted into purchase and habitual re-purchase action, and also into recommendation and effective feedback to us.

With the above process in mind, the starting point should be obvious: we should begin (if starting a new business) by looking at the different customers in the general market that we are trying to enter.

Customer Analysis

So, who is the customer? There are four main parties who constitute "the customer":

1. The User
The end-user should be the starting point. We need to know his or her tastes, behaviour patterns, wants, aspirations and underlying needs. Nuances should not be neglected as little things can prove powerful persuaders – or dissuaders.

Though an end-user may not enjoy senior status within the customer organisation, he may be a machine operator, for example, nonetheless, enlightened buyers or owners (see

122

below) will give great emphasis to what he wants. These lower-level operatives, through their evaluations, can mean the difference between success (ie a sale) or failure.

2. The Buyer
The buyer may not be the user. In addition to professional buyers (for retailers or wholesalers), there are others we will need to consider.

Take, for example, how underwear is bought and sold. Many men do not buy their own underwear – they may be too busy to do so, or they may have an aversion to shopping. Consequently, their wives will do the buying. This has profound implications as far as marketing focus is concerned. Price and distribution are likely to be important factors.

3. Gatekeepers
Trend-setters (such as actors and actresses) and opinion leaders fall into this category. Movie stars hold great sway over fashion trends. Gatekeepers such as secretaries should also be accommodated in order to gain access to decision makers. Spouses who accompany their partners shopping are often important gatekeepers and should thus be accorded due respect and care.

4. Owners
The 'owner', in this context, is the person who has the power to say yes or no. The Managing Director of a company may have to give his approval before a computer system can be purchased, even though he may know precious little about computers.

In analysing customers' needs and wants, a systematic identification and analysis of the parties mentioned above is a powerful source of inspiration and direction. Note, however:

123

- An individual may occupy one or more, or all, of the above roles.
- It is important to identify who *actually* possesses the main influence or power.
- Do not neglect personal (non-business) needs: for example, in selling a pay settlement to trade union representatives, remember that they need to look good before their constituents; thus, meeting this need may secure a smoother passage to a workable agreement.

Segmenting the Market

Segmentation is necessary to develop actual and perceived specialism. Once a segment has been selected, we can then dedicate our efforts and resources to developing competitive strength in that niche.

We choose our target segments through eliminating other segments of the market which are not attractive to us: those in decline or which require capabilities and resources which we do not possess.

Segmenting a market well requires substantial knowledge and skill – and generous doses of common sense (which as we all know is far from common). The unenlightened marketer will base his analysis purely on demographics: age group, location, sex, etc. More and more, analysts are looking into psychographics and the personalities of the target customers. Naturally, these more advanced techniques are incorporated with the more basic ones. Nonetheless, sophisticated marketing is becoming increasingly about in-depth and applied psychology.

Segmentation analysis should be carried out thoroughly so that, at the end, we would have identified the segment which is most attractive – and to which we are most suited. Servicing this market segment, therefore, then becomes our mission.

By focusing on just one segment (or a few very similar segments which can logically and practically be grouped into one for marketing purposes), we can then concentrate our resources on finding out:

- exactly what (e.g. product features, life-span, customer service, speed of delivery, convenience) is required by the customer;
- the price the customer will pay and whether this will enable us not only to survive, but to achieve our objectives of profit, growth and (maybe at a later stage when we are strong enough and ready) diversification;
- what is happening to our business environment, so that we can adapt quickly in order to be ready when the changes we have predicted actually do happen; this is proactive management and requires flexible and fast organisations, which in turn, require leaders with the same qualities.

The **Customer-led, Market-driven** approach is balanced and holistic, in that it endeavours to take into consideration all relevant perspectives and factors. It is not insular and self-centred. While its principal focus is on the customer, it always takes into account the capabilities and limitations of the organisation itself, and the opportunities and threats posed by factors which make up the environment in which the business is carried out (refer to the Comprehensive Analysis Programme in Chapter 2).

The very best global companies such as Singapore Airlines, 3M, Virgin, Honda and the like, adopt this orientation.

The Main Marketing Trends

While there are many, two crucial ones are:

1. Perceived Relative Quality (PRQ) – we have already discussed this, but it is so important that we will emphasise: we must (there is no alternative!) make *quality* and *value* as defined by our target customers, and as compared with those of our competitors, our absolute top priority!
2. Nobody, regardless of what is being offered, can afford to look on what is being offered as a mere product. It always has to be a product-service package, i.e. an amalgam of the primary product (or service) and the 'surround' service that adds true value to the primary product. In the main, the 'surround' service is the additional service that the customer perceives as being given for free.

With increasing competitiveness and rapidly increasing customer sophistication and awareness, the opportunity is here for the wise and brave to exploit this change through uncompromisingly superb customer service. The rule is to treat the customer as the MIP (Most Important Person).

One of the keys to making the customer feel that he is really special is to show him visibly that you are doing what your competitors are not doing: going out of your way to make life just that much better for him. The best salespeople have learnt that it's the little personal gestures, which hit the customer's soft spot, which really build positive impressions – and loyalty. These gestures, such as a thank you call, or a birthday card, can cost so little, be so simple and yet be so potent in positive impact.

If treated promptly and well, dissatisfied customers can be turned into better 'friends' than they would have been had there been no reason for dissatisfaction. Think of the opportunities to make lifelong collaborators and to win free, but powerful, 'word of mouth' advertising. Nothing persuades as strongly as genuine references from delighted customers.

VISIBLY DO WHAT YOUR COMPETITORS ARE NOT. THEREFORE GO OUT OF YOUR WAY TO MAKE LIFE JUST THAT MUCH BETTER (FOR THE CUSTOMER).

The downside is that well over 90% of customers who are dissatisfied do not complain – and most of these never come back. The average disgruntled customer will tell about nine others about his bad experience. Some will tell many more. But the really bad news is that the impact of one bad report is equal to twelve good ones!

To prove a point, I once made a trip to the USA and flew on an American carrier. The service was, to say the least, appalling – from check-in right through to the recovery of our battered suitcases (which we bought new in the States). Numerous other events (including rude and aggressive flight crew) helped detract from the otherwise lovely holiday. To date, I have related my horrific experience (identifying the airline by name) to over 2,000 people. No doubt, I will continue to cite this experience in future courses to illustrate the type of attitudes and behaviour that must be avoided like the plague!

Two Sundays after my return, I was sitting comfortably in church when, during his sermon, the preacher mentioned that he, too, had just returned from the USA and had found the very same airline 'the worst airline'. He solemnly promised that he would never fly with them again. In his case, however, he was addressing a congregation of over 1,000 people. No doubt he mentioned it at the earlier service, which is attended by close to that figure, as well. Imagine – in one morning, he 'spread the word' on which airline to avoid like "hell" to over 2,000 people . . . not counting those attending the two afternoon services!

The moral of the story is: make perfect customer service our goal. From this moment, let us train our people, motivate them and do everything to turn this ideal into reality. If we are already genuinely doing this, well done!

We need to encourage our customers to give us constructive feedback that we can act on. This means not just praise (which is useful as a measure of improvement and for morale boosting), but also complaints and suggestions for improvements. Encouraging customers means actively soliciting such feedback. Ways of making it easy, desirable, or costless for customers to provide feedback include:

- answering machines that record messages when the office is closed;
- telephone follow-ups to clients;
- signs placed strategically at entrances and exits, on labels, packaging;
- the use of assessment forms;
- strategically placed suggestion boxes, equipped with user-friendly forms and pens (in working order!);
- a freepost or freephone service;
- deploying well-trained customer liaison personnel;
- money-back guarantees for failure to satisfy;
- competitions.

The message to all our customers should be loud and clear:

> *If you are happy with us, please tell everyone (including us!) – otherwise just tell us and we will do everything possible to put things right!*

Training our staff to deal effectively with complaints (so they are turned into praises) and actually acting on *all* complaints is essential.

In this way we can convert our most disgruntled customers into our best friends.

Remember: the initiative to seek feedback, and to act on it, must be wholly ours – because we are the ones who wish to remain in business!

Developing a Marketing Strategy

Let us recap. From the vision we get a mission. From the mission, we are able to set corporate objectives. However, these corporate objectives must be developed by fully considering information that is revealed through, among other things, a SWOT analysis.

SWOT stands for Strengths, Weaknesses, Opportunities and Threats. Properly researched and executed, this is a powerful approach to evaluating what business we ought to be in, what we should be doing, and how we should be doing it. It is *vital* that this analysis examines as many relevant viewpoints as possible – beginning, of course, with the customer's. In carrying out the SWOT analysis, we must resist relying solely on our own opinions. Believe it or not, whatever we think will be of little consequence if our customers see things differently!

Once, after accepting a major contract to provide in-depth strategic consultancy for a new client, I immediately faxed through instructions to my associates in London to undertake a research of the global opportunities and threats relating to the industry concerned. Two of our new consultants were horrified at my request. One of them, who had just received his MBA, protested that the research should begin from within, looking at the strengths and weaknesses of the organisation first.

Think about why I asked for an *outside-in* approach. This was an established 'blue chip' company that wanted to ensure that it was going in the right direction and doing the right things. Beginning a strategic review from within the organisation has a disturbing tendency to limit strategic options and creative, unencumbered thinking. An *inside-out* investigation will reveal operational matters that need to be improved. Once exposed, the temptation to improve these, rather than evaluate whether they are the right activities, becomes difficult to resist. The tendency is to perpetuate activities, even though those activities may entail substantial opportunity costs.

Brainstorming, marketing and operational research, and Comprehensive Analysis Programme techniques can add much to the SWOT analysis. Through a creative cocktail of appropriate techniques, highly valuable insights into the strengths and weaknesses of ourselves and our competitors can be attained. Appropriate marketing strategies may then be developed.

Even though we have researched all relevant information, and have made our forecasts for the future, things may not turn out as planned. Thus, well managed, forward-looking organisations will prepare contingency plans.

A strategic marketing plan is nothing less than a *war plan*. In war, it is necessary to try to forecast the conditions which will prevail in the arena at different stages of the campaign. The leading generals must also attempt, through in-depth analysis of the tactics used by the enemy, to think like the enemy and, therefore, predict the enemy's actions, manoeuvres, and reactions.

Powerful computers are used to play war games. These games simulate likely environmental states and conditions. The outcomes of the battles, given different hypothetical scenarios, are predicted, so that battle plans can be developed and tested. With business planning models with simulation facilities becoming so cheaply available, even smaller businesses may benefit from these techniques.

I once read an article by a British management consultant in which he stated: '*Strategies never won a battle! Tactics win battles.*' The strategists of the commercial world today often develop *strategies* without due consideration of the *tactics* that must be deployed to implement the strategies successfully.

The message is clear: involve the line managers and even the 'foot soldiers' who will have to carry out the tactical implementation of business strategies. These people probably know the current state of affairs on the 'front line' better than anyone else. They can provide rich insights which could avoid much waste of time, money and goodwill!

In short, therefore, let us try *genuine* participation in conceptualisation, design, development, implementation, monitoring and review. Companies that have conscientiously and intelligently used this approach have been consistently superior not only in the design of systems and solutions, but also in achieving more effective communication which leads to better teamwork, morale and performance.

The Marketing Mix

The elements of the marketing mix are interactive. Consequently, developing the analysis must be an **iterative** process.

The marketing mix is composed of four interlinked and interdependent strategies relating to:

- Product (including service and production)
- Price
- Place (distribution)
- Promotion and Advertising.

All four P's must be considered in developing or changing the marketing strategy.

The marketing mix is developed from strategic analysis, including a marketing audit to identify opportunities in the market place. The skilful and innovative marketer will look for opportunities in events that others see to be threats.

For example, Japanese car manufacturers were careful,

when making their entry into the US car market, not to collide headlong into the likes of General Motors, Ford or Chrysler. They understood that for a smaller combatant (as they were then), the best strategy would be to avoid conflict and to avoid being noticed by the giants. They successfully achieved this by using a method known as *counter-cannibalism*. By concentrating on the small family saloon car (which was neglected by the big American car manufacturers), the Japanese were able to develop their reputation for cost-efficiency and quality. This was helped along by the 1974 oil crisis, which gave much grief to the manufacturers and owners of the thirsty, large-engined American cars. Thus, a major threat to the American car industry was exploited as a golden opportunity by Japanese car and motorcycle manufacturers – not only in the USA, but all around the world. Small proved beautiful!

To illustrate the need to take into account all four P's, perhaps we can liken the marketing strategy to a rope. With this rope we will pull the business uphill to a given destination: our ultimate, long-term corporate objective. We will pass visible landmarks – milestones – along the way. These interim targets must be quantifiable. The rope is woven from four cords: the four P's. Without any one of these cords, the rope will lack the necessary strength, and may snap. If this happens, the company will be sent rolling downhill, away from its destination.

Product Strategy
Let us recapitulate on two important lessons:

- People buy solutions.
- Increasingly, the way to keep customers happy is not just to offer top-quality *products* (this applies even to service organisations such as lawyers, accountants and hairdressers) but to offer first-class customer *service* that makes the customer realise beyond the shadow of a doubt that he is our Most Important Person.

Our business strategy must, therefore, be to:

- develop the products that the target customers will really want to buy;
- deliver them when the customer wants them;
- through excellent customer service keep the customer for life!

In Chapter Four, I told the story of my recent visit to a nearby chain store. The service – from management to check-out operator – was appalling. In contrast, I had quite a different experience when I visited Wing Yip, a Chinese supermarket in north London. The store is renowned for the great variety and high quality of its products. But what really impresses customers is the standard of its customer service.

Wing Yip, although a large and extremely popular supermarket, has only two checkout stations. Both are equipped with basic cash registers, not computerised ones, yet there are seldom any queues. The reason becomes obvious when one witnesses the Wing Yip 'A-team' in action.

Each station is operated by a team of three. An attendant unloads articles from the trolley onto the counter. The cashier then rings up the purchases while yet another attendant packs and loads them onto another trolley. The customer does not have to lift a finger throughout this amazing, precision operation – it took them two minutes to clear my fully loaded trolley and to process my payment!

What has Wing Yip that British supermarkets don't? It boils down to motivation, culture, and training.

Product strategy covers everything about the product: the actual product, its packaging, customer service, after-sales service, delivery, etc. It also includes factors often not given enough serious attention: the brand name and logo – vital components of the corporate image. The name Wing Yip, to the initiated, means quality, value for money and superb service.

It is essential that the total product/service package is compatible with the desired image; there should be no weak links. Even seemingly innocuous or minor deficiencies can cause serious damage to the prospects of the product, and to the organisation: i.e. affecting all other product ranges.

Brand names are vital because customers use them to identify what they want and also what they don't. Brand names also play a vital part in actually creating an image, and/or promoting the product. Other tactics that can promote a distinctive image include:

- clear, distinctive brand names;
- attractive (and in the case of shirts and underwear, physically non-irritating) labels;
- use of serial numbers or artist's signatures to highlight exclusivity;
- better packaging.

The serious marketer is constantly reviewing his approach and operations to ensure that his product/service amalgam is as close to the perfect solution to his customers' needs as possible. Some questions that will need to be answered are:

- What, why, where and how does he buy?
- What are the product features he values?
- What are his priorities?
- Can we attach monetary values to different product features?

The sharp-end analysis must be forward looking:

- Are products viable?
- Is the market growing, stagnating or declining?

- How long will the trend last? (This will impact on Research and Development to develop replacement products.)
- What are the implications for re-training and new capital investment?
- What are the strategic implications to the competition and to our own existing product lines?
- Can we afford to diversify in this way?

These are just a few questions we have to consider in analysing products. Initiate the search for answers by involving people with different relevant perspectives in brainstorming.

Asking the right questions frequently enough is crucial to sustained competitiveness.

In knowledge building, it is good to remember Rudyard Kipling's advice:

> *I keep six honest serving men,*
> *They taught me all I know,*
> *Their names are What?*
> *and Why? and When?,*
> *and How? and Where? and Who?*

I would add: listen first to *Who* . . . he will help identify the others.

Pricing Strategy

The right product may be priced wrongly. If this is so, the anticipated sales may not happen.

Regardless of quality, pricing is important. This is especially vital if the price level wanders too far beyond the upper or lower limits associated with the relevant market niche.

We must re-emphasise, however, that quality is something customers are willing to dig deeper into their pockets for.

It is occasionally possible, given the right circumstances, to create an image of the company or product in the mind of the customer that makes it unique, in which case customers will be less inclined to compare prices with 'substitutes'. If the company or product is perceived to be unique, to the customer there will be no substitutes! Such a strategy is often risky.

Unless the appeal to the customer can be sustained, the product will suffer the fate suffered by so many fads which disappear after a blazing start. Notwithstanding this word of warning, many fads have provided funds for projects and businesses which have gone on to be *sustainably* successful. In such instances, the product is in fact a 'cash cow' with a planned, short life-cycle.

There are always exceptions to the rules – and pricing guidelines are no exception to the exceptions.

Consider the economist's traditional downward-sloping demand curve: the higher the price, the lower the demand. This can sometimes·be avoided by skilful marketing based on a clear focus and concentration of all resources and effort on the specific market segment being targeted. Consequently, it is quite possible to sell more by charging higher prices, assuming that the rest of the marketing mix supports the premium-pricing strategy.

Example:
Britvic produces fruit juice in small cans. The company ran into problems, and was put up for sale. The buyer turned the business around by re-positioning the product as a mixer (far less competition) rather than a soft drink (lots of juices on offer). The re-positioning essentially involved three things: first, the packaging (the design on the tin) was changed;

second, the price was increased substantially, and third, distribution focused on pubs, bars and restaurants. Because the image that resulted was classier and more attractive, sales (and profits) soared; today Britvic is offered in the majority of pubs and bars in Britain!

Bohemian crystal has the same potential for re-positioning. In fact, its image is chequered internationally: distinctly better in some markets than others. Prices are still generally lower than comparable crystal produced in the West because, historically, the cost of production has always been cheaper in Eastern Europe. As price is often associated directly with quality, the fact that Czech crystal is lower priced is perceived to be an admission of lower quality.

Nevertheless, Czech glass and crystal compete very favourably both on price and image in certain countries. In Singapore, Bohemian crystal is seen to be upmarket and is sold in the best retail outlets at prices comparable to those for crystal produced by the English and other Europeans. This is perhaps attributable to the capability of the Singapore firms which have been responsible for marketing the product.

Price setting methods

(a) Cost-Plus (Mark up)

As the name suggests, this involves adding on a profit element to the basic cost of the product or service.

Many garages still use this method, and so we will use this business to illustrate:

	£
Labour (3 hours @ £25)	75.00
Parts	95.00
Direct cost	170.00

Apportioned overhead (@ £10 per labour hour)	30.00
Total Cost	200.00
Add: mark up required (35%)	70.00
Net Price	270.00
Add: VAT @ 17.5%	47.25
TOTAL	317.25

The advantage of the cost-plus method is that it is simple to implement. The great and serious disadvantage is that, on its own, it ignores the customer and the competition – the two most important factors in any marketing strategy.

(b) Margin (Marginal Pricing)

An improvement on cost-plus, this method involves finding a price that will enable us to be competitive and sell enough to meet our objectives. Thus, with the cost-plus method, the starting point is actual cost; with marginal pricing, we start from the *end* price and work backwards.

To illustrate, say a Czech suit manufacturer is planning to enter the London retail market. His target segment is the young male city professional. He establishes that, on average, retailers work on a mark-up of 175% (nett of Value Added Tax). He has identified the best retail outlets to secure his goals relating to image and sales volume. He finds that comparable Italian-made suits retail at between £230 and £285. After research and discussions with retailers, he assesses that for the first year, a 12.5% retail discount will be required, and that retailers will want a 200% mark-up.

His budget computations will be structured along the following lines:

	£ Low end	£ High end
Gross price of comparable Italian suit	230.00	285.00
Less VAT (Gross × 17.5/117.5)	(34.26)	(42.45)
Net Price (of comparable Italian suit)	195.74	242.55
Less: retail discount (12.5%)	(24.47)	(30.32)
Net Price of Czech suit	171.27	212.23
Less: retailer's mark up (2/3)	(114.18)	(141.49)
Price received from retailer	57.09	70.74
Less: Insurance and freight (say 10% CIF)	(5.71)	(7.07)
Ex-factory plus Sales Tax	51.38	63.67
Less: Sales Tax (say 20%)	(10.28)	(12.73)
Ex-factory price	41.10	50.94
Less: Margin required (20%)*	(8.22)	(10.19)
Total cost budgeted**	32.88	40.75

Notes:
* A margin (on sales value – in this case, on the ex-factory price) of 20% is equivalent to a mark-up (which is based on cost) of 25%.
** The budget allowed for total cost must then be divided among the various direct and indirect costs of the operation.

In principle, the marginal-pricing approach is the more market-oriented of the two methods covered thus far, in that by starting from a viable price, the method takes into account the influences of the customers (retailer and end-buyer) as well as competitors.

In practice, the two methods can be used to complement each other. The marginal method should initiate the analysis: it sets a starting point for the budgeting process. The cost-plus method, working out componental costs in sufficient detail, will establish the feasibility of the proposition, and will also throw light on relevant parameters of the decision such as sales volume or areas where cost saving is possible (e.g. using alternative methods of transportation).

Even the marginal-pricing method is inadequate as it does not tailor what is being offered to the precise requirements of the customer. The intermediate customer (distributor), and not just the end buyer or user, is also an important party. Top-quality distributors, such as Marks and Spencer, are highly selective and extremely demanding. They are fully aware of their superior bargaining position, which is due to the value that their name adds to the prestige of a product or supplier.

(c) Value Analysis

Because the true champions will always seek new ways to differentiate themselves and to increase their competitive edge, one of their preoccupations is the enhancement of their knowledge of their customers – and ways of applying that superior knowledge in their operations.

The Japanese improved on traditional pricing methods with their development of Value Analysis.

As the term suggests, the method involves, first, the breaking up of solutions (products and services) into components (colour, features, size, durability, safety, guarantee, convenience of distribution, and so on) and attempting to place values, from the perspective of the customer, on those individual components. The next step is to work out total values by aggregating componental values. Thus, prices for various models of products can be set with greater precision.

The Japanese have long practised product analysis in their own product development. They began their post-war boom by buying some 10,000 licences from the Americans, as well as by aggressively acquiring and analysing the products of competitors – and borrowing ideas and patterns for their own products. Though the latter was a practice deemed unethical, it was not least through this approach that the modern foundations of their world-beating, durable customer goods industries were set.

Value Analysis does what the other, earlier methods failed to do. It not only improves understanding of the consumer's value system, it also integrates product (including service) development together with distribution, promotion, and, of course, pricing: a truly integrated marketing mix.

(d) Value Engineering

As with Value Analysis, this method deals not just with price – but all the four P's.

Just as marginal pricing and the cost-plus approaches start from opposite ends of the equation, Value Engineering is really the reverse of Value Analysis. Value Analysis begins with a study of what exists. Value Engineering starts from what does *not* yet exist.

Value Engineering begins by researching what the target customer values. The focus is on needs and the resulting wants: wants which may be subliminal and not consciously realised by the customer because the solutions do not yet exist. Much of the research is, thus, focused on developing an insight into the fantasies and wishes of the customer.

Once the product has been endowed with features that satisfy the customer's needs, wants and fantasies, the components and then the total product are valued and priced using Value Analysis methods.

When the Japanese introduced the world's first plain-paper fax-photocopier, they answered the unspoken prayer of many businesses operating in high-cost premises, who had to photocopy faxes received, and hold stocks of expensive fax paper in already crowded premises. This machine, like the Honda Civic, was the product of Value Engineering.

By applying Value Engineering successfully, a business can help ensure that its product is on the market before others have even begun product development. Thus, the innovator is able to enjoy the early weeks, months or even years to skim the market as a virtual monopolist, recovering initial outlay, so that prices can be lowered, just as the competitors enter with their substitutes.

Value Engineering is, thus, a powerful tool for achieving effective speed. The underpinning principle, which can be used in various circumstances, is that instead of following, we should exploit our creativity and strengths to engineer changes that we can then exploit before anybody else is in the position to do so. This attitude requires courage and an opportunistic approach, but, to quote the favourite admonition of a colleague:

To faith add wisdom.

The methods of pricing, and of marketing, we adopt will largely be dependent upon our attitudes, talent, preparation, and circumstances. Instead of following, we can lead. This option is naturally more risky than following – but the rewards can be substantial.

In practice, each of the four methods can be used in conjunction with the others. Prices set by Value Engineering and Value Analysis can be used to verify viability and to develop operational budgets using marginal costing. The cost-plus method can then be used to verify feasibility.

Constantly falling hardware prices and the proliferation of powerful, user-friendly software are making computer-aided scenario planning accessible to many businesses. Consequently, businesses should, if they have yet to do so, take time from their fire-fighting activities to research the ways in which their cost control, effectiveness, speed, and productivity can be improved with state-of-the-art technology. If these opportunities are not grasped and if they fail to launch themselves onto this learning curve soon, their competitors will.

Market testing

What is developed in the laboratory or design studio cannot be guaranteed to work in the real world. The newer or more altered a product is, the more important that market tests should be conducted.

The trials should not be restricted to test marketing after the product or concept has been finalised, as this can prove prohibitive to change if the tests at such a late stage show that there are serious defects. Instead, tests should be carried out throughout the development of the product. Naturally, the bigger the investment, the more thorough the testing and product development control should be.

Prototypes, retailer surveys, systems walk-throughs, user trials, concept analysis by target customers and area test marketing are some techniques that can, and should, be used to evaluate the marketing strategy – and the investment.

Economising on research is often a sure recipe for disaster. If common sense is applied in adequate doses, research need not be costly. Research is always educational; even if it proves that initial assumptions were correct, peace of mind is a valuable gain.

When it comes to advisors and consultants, be wary: not all will be competent. Look out for logical inconsistencies, unproven assumptions, factual omissions, failure to consider the obvious, and for ulterior motives.

Place Strategy

This 'P' has already been touched upon, but we shall now elaborate.

Distribution is the process that gets the completed product or service to the customer. In manufacturing, it is the physical transfer process from the factory or warehouse to the customer (and sometimes, back from the customer to the factory . . . and then back again . . .).

We saw in the case history above that distribution *focus* was important for Britvic. It was one of the vital strands of the strategy that turned it around from being a loser into a roaring success. The reason that Britvic is sold in bars and not generally in supermarkets is that consumers are more price conscious when shopping: they would rather get four times the quantity of fruit juice for the same amount of money!

Distribution covers wholesalers, retailers, agencies, and direct sales (mail order or sales representatives calling direct). A very important aspect of how customers buy is where the products should be placed so that:

- they will be noticed frequently by the target customer;
- the customer is most likely to buy.

As with the other four P's, the distribution outlets must be the ones most suitable for that particular category of customer. For example, exclusive artwork should not be sold through down-market outlets.

Although the outlets must be the right ones for the desired image, and to attract the right customers, distributors are often very choosy. For example, the professional buyers for Harrods are notorious for the very challenging quality standards they impose. Winning shelf space in many distribution outlets can be a harrowing affair. The onus of proving that carrying the product will be a highly worthwhile investment for the distributor is on the supplier. Often the distributor will insist on substantial advertising and promotion from the supplier before providing shelf-space for new products. This is yet another strong reason for focusing on developing a quality reputation and brand name.

Quality and value are the key elements for success – not only in the home market, but also in a global context. The world is increasingly becoming a single market. Unless we act fast and appropriately, we will certainly lose out to the competition. Globalisation must be a key part of any firm's marketing plan.

Promotion Strategy

In sophisticated markets where choice is great, promotion and advertising are areas in which the battle is fiercest. The key lies in convincing the customer that the product/service being promoted will meet his needs better than any other comparable solution.

The strategic objective of promotion and advertising are to:

- turn a prospect into a customer;
- turn the new customer into a habitual customer;
- get him to try other products;
- turn him into a walking, breathing advertising campaign (word-of-mouth advertising is the most persuasive form);
- get him to provide feedback for sustaining constant improvement.

Before continuing, let us distinguish between *promotion* and *advertising*. The differences are principally technical. In modern parlance the two terms are used interchangeably.

Promotion is about inducing trial. Promotion usually gives the target customer an incentive to 'taste'; for example, free tasting in supermarkets to promote a new range of Californian wines or discount coupons on catfood to stimulate purchase.

The aims of promotion are to stimulate:

- new customers to try an existing product;
- former customers to re-try an existing or 'improved' product;
- existing customers to try a new product;
- new customers to try a new product.

Advertising is about *maintaining* or increasing the sale of an existing product.

Free offers and similar inducements are not normally included in pure advertising campaigns. However, the distinction is sometimes blurred. Consider for example, campaigns relating to existing products. When competition is fierce, and free gifts or inducements are incorporated into the campaign, the distinction between advertising and promotion almost disappears.

Such combined campaigns can be highly effective and far safer than outright price reduction. The latter tactic is risky: customers may be unhappy about paying the normal price once the discounts are removed or a price war may result, which can be devastating not only to individual firms but to the industry as a whole.

There are various conceptual models which attempt to explain the stage-by-stage objectives of an advertising campaign. One model is AIDA – an acronym which stands for:

- Awareness
- Interest
- Desire
- Action

Some campaigns comprise a single advertisement or similar advertisements designed to achieve the same Action from the target customers: buy!

Others are more subtle and sophisticated, and usually more expensive. The first phase might be to get attention; the second, interest or curiosity (e.g. send for free information); the third, desire. The final phase should stimulate the action that was the strategic objective of the campaign.

Some advertisers have succeeded only in frustrating their target customers by bringing them to the 'desire' stage only to leave them disappointed because the action they want to take cannot be taken. A classic example is where advertisers fail to provide details of where or how the product can be obtained! Such shoddy advertising can prove disastrously counter-productive.

Because image is important in influencing purchase (and repurchase) behaviour, companies pay tremendous amounts to create an image appealing to their target customers through 'role model' association, for example, Pepsi Cola's use of people like Michael Jackson, Madonna, and Tina Turner. This phenomenon is especially true in the FMCG (fast moving consumer goods) market where the focus is on the young and susceptible.

Another conceptual model which seeks to explain the staged objectives of advertising is the ATR model:

- Attention
- Trial
- Reinforcement

ATR emphasises *repurchase* behaviour: customer loyalty.

What both have in common is the first step: Attention. Most people tend to forget advertisements. Only 10%, on average, are able to remember an advertisement after a month or so and even then, the association is likely to be hazy. Reinforcement is, therefore, vital to sustain profitable growth.

While it is essential that the advertising conveys the desired image, for it to be memorable, there should be preferably only one message. Any more would be 'overkill', which often annoys the customer, or confuses him (or both!). The message should be clear and powerful, so that real impact is made and that the advertising is not easily forgotten.

This may give the impression that advertising is a discipline that is clear cut. However, the most important thing about advertising is that it needs to be impactful and positively stimulating. Consequently, creativity is vital. Boredom, commonality, and confusion, are perceptions to avoid. We should never rush out an advertisement that is not going to enhance our image.

Remember: no advert at all is better than a bad one.

It should be noted that creative advertising, which may say little (or sometimes nothing at all) about the product may still prove extremely effective because it causes target customers to associate positively with the product.

For example, one Heineken poster showed a stretch of the M25 (the busiest motorway in Britain) absolutely free of all traffic – save for a Heineken truck. At the foot of the poster was the famous legend: Only Heineken can do this (!).

Although nobody is likely to be convinced that Heineken can clear the M25, the image is clear: Heineken is for fun people, typically youngish professionals leading very hectic and stressful lives, whose highpoint of the day may be a relaxing time at the local pub after work.

Advertising campaigns are often very expensive affairs. Often this is due to the fact that the advertiser does not know his customer well enough, and/or is not using the most effective and cost-effective ways of getting the customer's attention. In the case of media advertising, checks on the effective audience penetration should be made. However, where the product is something not bought frequently, such as a car, advertising may 'sow the seeds' which will take some time to germinate and to translate into actual sales. Expectations should, therefore, be realistic from the start to avoid unwarranted disillusionment.

With the right information about our target customer – which magazines and newspapers does he read?, what types of TV programmes or movies does he watch? – we can then directly market to him using the right media, including mailshots.

It would be irresponsible not to reiterate that overkill should be avoided. It should also be remembered that people buy solutions to their needs/problems. In addition, unless first impressions are favourable and highlight the benefits to the customer, he is unlikely to finish reading or watching the advertisement.

The worst thing to do is to *overpromise and underdeliver*. This happens, for example, when an advertising campaign is highly successful, perhaps too successful, and plenty of orders are received. It then happens that some of the orders cannot be met because of stock deficiency! What does this achieve? The loss of credibility and a bad reputation.

It is far better to *underpromise* and *overdeliver*.

Nevertheless, some creative advertisers deliberately promise what they cannot deliver – and then exploit the opportunity. To illustrate, a common practice is to place newspaper advertisements for a new product. Due to holding costs and uncertainty as to the customer response, the trader will order or produce a conservative quantity. Should the response be in excess of stock, the trader will: exaggerate the amount sold; be sickly sweet to the customer (who should be by now feeling quite upset at having missed the opportunity); insist on placing the customer's order for the next shipment so that disappointment will not happen a second time. This exploits the principle that if a disappointed customer's problem is dealt with swiftly and to his satisfaction, he is more likely to re-purchase than if there had been no disappointment to start with.

Another useful tip is that people enjoy pleasant surprises, such as receiving free gifts, or products or services that exceed their expectations. Salespeople should always plan and do things that bring good feelings to their customers. Such acts can involve little or no out of pocket costs, like a friendly non-business related phone call, a birthday card or gift, or recommending a customer to the customer. Thank you's for orders placed are always nice to receive.

Keeping the Customer for life!

It is substantially cheaper to service existing clients than to get new ones. By getting to know existing clients really well, innovative organisations are able to adapt their product/ services to the continually changing needs and tastes of their customers. By consistently demonstrating that 'the customer is boss', we will continue to delight the customer – and if the customer is delighted, he will have little reason to go elsewhere. Consequently, this will save us money, time and distractive effort, the benefits of which can be passed back to the customer. Thus, it becomes yet another ongoing Win-Win cycle.

Changing Marketing Strategies and Risk Management

A **market** can be defined by:

- demographics, i.e. income group, social class, age, sex, occupation, location, etc;
- purchase behaviour, i.e. point of purchase, distribution channels used;
- type of use, i.e. reason for purchase.

Note that customers may have different purchase behaviours depending on circumstances. While most of us may do the majority of our shopping at supermarkets, we use the local store for fast purchases and small quantities (like when the flour runs out).

There are four broad strategies in marketing. They are represented in the marketing matrix below:

MARKET PENETRATION	MARKET DEVELOPMENT
* Existing Product * Existing Market	* Existing Product * New Market
PRODUCT DEVELOPMENT	DIVERSIFICATION
* New Product * Existing Market	* New Product * New Market

Entrepreneurs are by definition risk-takers. Inexperienced entrepreneurs often make the mistake of diversifying – starting a new business can be considered diversifying – before they are ready. This may explain the extremely high rate of business failure in most market economies.

To help avoid failure, there are two cardinal rules that business people would do well to apply:

- Do not move except from a position of strength (unless one has no choice due to unforeseeable circumstances).
- Timing is critical: an army that moves at the right time can secure victory against a much greater host.

In applying these principles to the marketing matrix, it should be evident that the safest strategy is **Market Penetration**: we do more of what we have always been doing where we have always been doing it!

Market Development is normally the next safest as it usually involves less capital investment and is less entangling than developing new products, i.e. **Product Development**. Product Development is risky because if the new products are not of the same high quality as existing products, customers may get the impression that the supplier has deteriorated. Thus, with the same dirty broad brush, existing products will be tarred. Regrettable, but true: it is far easier to damage a reputation than to build one up.

The riskiest strategy is that of **Diversification**. Diversification can seriously weaken existing strengths, more severely than mere product development.

Arguments given for product development and diversification are often based on the **portfolio theory**: it is dangerous to put all the eggs in one basket. This is certainly logical, but unless one is absolutely certain of the general success of the move or investment, one should have sufficient provision to accommodate the potential failure. In short, should the unspeakable happen, the damage must be withstandable.

Risk-reducing techniques include:

- syndication;
- involving other partners;
- cutting down the initial scale of a large project.

Syndicating or bringing in other risk-taking partners will often do more than reduce the cost burden on a per capita basis: synergy may also develop if the expectations of results are clear, and the partners are culturally compatible. Naturally, loss of control and difficulties resulting from having to work with others should also be considered to balance the analysis.

Businesses, especially new ones, need as a priority to build up a cash reserve as a financial buffer which will see them through the lean times should their change in marketing strategy go wrong, or should unforeseen obstacles and delays arise. The reason this is so important is that financial pressure, if the buffer is inadequate or nonexistent, will often result in panic measures and loss of direction. Many potentially viable businesses have been torpedoed in this way.

154

Undercapitalisation, resulting from over-optimism, poor planning, and/or inexperience, has sunk many a business.

Notwithstanding this cautious advice, the riskiest strategy beyond the short term is *no* change. Without innovation and improvement, no business will remain competitive for long.

As globalisation should always be planned for, a safe route for expansion should include Market Development. A step by step approach may be as follows:

Phase **Strategic Action**

1   Market Penetration either alone or combined with Market Development.
       This defend plus attack approach may be superior where the business is able to do so without undue risk; where critical mass is an important factor; or some other extenuating factor exists, e.g. contractual obligations or necessity in face of foreign competition in domestic markets.

2   Develop new markets.
       Faced with the unknown, a cautious start may be advisable. Testing the market through export using local agents avoids heavy initial outlay. If the venture proves successful, subsequent investment can then be financed from the cash flow generated, and cheaper finance obtained due to the positive track record.

3   Develop new products.
       By this time new markets will no longer be new, vital experience having been gathered in the interim period. The funding advantages available in Phase 2 should also be accessible at this stage due to an established reputation.

4   Finally, when very strong financially and in relevant experience (this and know-how may be bought in) diversification may be desirable. This is not mandatory and many businesses become globally successful without ever diversifying. Nevertheless, the world is a big place for expansion, and global synergy can be very rewarding.

Conclusion

Marketing begins with analysing our ability in the context of the environment, not least of all the dynamic nature of competition. Nonetheless, the more we know of the customer, and the closer we are to him, the stronger our competitive position will be. By consistently delighting the customer, we will be able to keep him from looking for alternative suppliers.

Because the marketing mix must be integrated, none of the four P's should be looked at or developed in isolation. It is essential that the total marketing mix is developed to fit in well with our SWOT analysis, and that all the strategies and tactics that are developed from it are focused on clearly defined objectives, which are in turn based on the company's ultimate goals. As always, we have to quantify our strategies to ensure that we have enough money, time and resources to make the marketing strategy succeed.

As the world is becoming increasingly volatile, constant reviews of the strategy we adopt need to be undertaken. The foundation of strategy should always be a customer-directed vision.

Failure to budget well (especially cash flows) can not only doom the strategy, but might completely torpedo the entire organisation. The failure rate for new businesses within the first three years in the UK is over 90%! This is despite numerous government schemes to help new business initiatives.

The moral of the story is: research and plan thoroughly before acting. Acting without a firm foundation of knowledge is folly. Japanese companies have much lower project failure rates than either the British or Americans because they are very thorough in their analysis, believe in comprehensive planning, and do not believe in taking action until there remains very little uncertainty. All this preparatory activity makes eventual implementation swift and successful.

Worth bearing in mind: good marketing makes selling a whole lot easier and cheaper. If the product/service is the best, from the perspective of the customer, then he will buy; we will not have to 'hard sell'. This, naturally, enables life to be more enjoyable for all parties concerned!

Let us not be hasty and impulsive. Before we begin doing things correctly, let us make sure that we are doing the right things. Without a clear and empowering vision to set the strategic course, we will go astray. Learning is, thus, crucial to survival and prosperity.

It is a fool who insists on learning from his own mistakes – when he can learn from those of others.
Old Chinese Proverb.

EPILOGUE

We began by emphasising the need for a strong corporate vision: a fire which consumes all negativism and which replaces doubts with inspiration, unity, energy, focus, and confidence.

We conclude therefore, by returning to the starting point. Success and prosperity begin with a conducive mentality – a positive attitude. The seeds of success are, thus, first of all sown in our minds.

For these seeds to germinate, flourish and bear rich fruit, they must be protected and nurtured. Top managers are the ultimate custodians of the corporate vision. Nobody can replace them as the principal catalyst.

Many of the lessons discussed in this book are not mine, but have been gleaned from the written and verbal experiences of winners and losers. Successes and failure – and not only our own – are powerful teachers if we would but learn.

Some truths are obvious, as they lie on the surface or close to it. Others are buried, and to see these truths in their entirety, we need to probe deeply. To be unique, we need to go far beyond the superficial. Most people are content with seeing only the superficial: as a result, they end up being mediocre.

Again and again, we need to encourage ourselves and our people to be unique. We need to differentiate ourselves by not conforming to existing standards and limitations. There must be no compromise on excellence and competitiveness. There must be the courage to aspire to outperform the competition – to the extent that they will not be seen as even in the same race. Delusions and complacency must be laid aside, the competition is uncharitable and vicious. *Only the fittest will survive.*

In the race for survival, there are only two ways to avoid being crowded out by the other runners. The first is to be ahead of the rest. The other is to be left behind.

Which will we choose? The second choice is easy but, ultimately, fatal. The first, on the other hand, is initially painful, but ultimately rewarding. As bodybuilders say, 'No pain, no gain.'

> *To learn and know is one thing,*
> *but to learn and do is better,*
> *however, at the end of the day,*
> *the only thing that matters,*
> *is that we have learnt, known, acted,*
> *and (most importantly) achieved.*

Never has it been truer than now, to say that we are not rewarded by how hard we try – we are only rewarded according to results. It is, thus, imperative that we think well before we sweat: productivity comes through working smart, and certainly not just by working hard.

Dr Quek may be contacted at:

SynerGem Europe Ltd
61 Castle Avenue, Ewell, Surrey KT17 2PJ, England
Tel: (081) 786 7624   Fax: (081) 786 7623

SynerGem Prague s.r.o.
Žitná 6, 120 00 Praha 2, Czech Republic
Tel: (+42 2) 6631 2640/1   Fax: (+42 2) 6631 2642

The Chicken manager

The chicken manager is contented – even happy – to remain in a protected environment. He does not venture out of his compound. Little does he realise that what keeps the competition and threats out also imprisons and weakens him. As such, he grows fat and complacent. Within his protected market, the chicken manager fails to see the predators outside who are growing stronger by the day – and creeping ever so much nearer to his *territory*.

When the time comes, the chicken is slaughtered and eaten – all without warning and fight!

The *parable* here is: market protectionism is only acceptable if it is to be scaled down and eliminated over the short to medium term (no longer than *really* necessary) to enable the "protected" businesses or industries to develop their competitive abilities during that period of grace. Politically, protectionism is also often useful, if used effectively, to negotiate trade concessions and bilateral deals. However, governments that foolishly hold on to protectionism, regardless of good intentions, do their country's businesses no favours. The latter become *battery hens* as a result! When the trade barriers fall (as they inevitably will), such "protected" local businesses will not be equipped to compete to an environment where the "law of the jungle" – *survival of the fittest* – prevails.

UNLIKELY, BUT TRUE
(A Bureaucratic Tale)

Once upon a time, it was resolved to have a boat race between a Japanese team and a team representing the N.H.S. Both teams practised long and hard to reach their peak performance. On the big day they were as ready as they could be. The Japanese won by a mile.

Afterwards the N.H.S. team became very discouraged by the result and morale sagged. Senior management decided that the reason for the crushing defeat had to be found and a working party was set up to investigate the problem and recommend appropriate action.

Their conclusion was that the Japanese team had eight people rowing and one person steering, whereas the N.H.S. team had eight people steering and one person rowing.

Senior Management immediately hired a consultancy company to do a study on the team's structure. Millions of pounds and several months later they concluded that "too many people were steering and not enough rowing".

To prevent losing to the Japanese next year, the team structure was changed to three "Assistant Steering Managers", three "Steering Managers", one "Executive Steering Manager" and a "Director of Steering Services". A performance and appraisal system was set up to give the person rowing the boat more incentive to work harder.

The next year the Japanese won by two miles. The N.H.S. laid off the rower for poor performance, sold off all the paddles, cancelled all capital investment for new equipment and halted development of a new canoe. The money saved was used to fund higher than average pay awards to Senior Management.

Anonymous

INVESTING IN THE CZECH REPUBLIC

Arguably, after the Slovak Republic, which I feel has even more exciting potential for medium to long-term investment (particularly for the "Johnny-come-lately" Asian investors), the Czech Republic is probably *the* best place for investment in Central and Eastern Europe. Still, there is much to be sustained and extended, if the momentum of regional, as well as global change is to be effectively exploited.

I shall first address a few of the principal pitfalls that frequently frustrate the unwary investor. While I am writing to forewarn the latter, my message is also directed at the decision makers and influential gatekeepers in the Czech public sector, quasi-governmental institutions, trade associations and in the private sector. For they are the ones who have the power to change things as they are, and who will be, to varying degrees, the architects of the future. My hope is that they will finally decide to apply their authority to bring about necessary corrections. Without these changes, which are in the main attitudinal in nature, the transformation of the Czech Republic into a true regional centre of excellence will be slow and tortuous.

The brand of protectionism being practised here is of an insidious and self-destructive type. In due course, unless a radical turnabout occurs, it will devastate many businesses and even whole industry sectors. Such damage will be unnecessary, unjustifiable and a great loss to the nation. The lack of enforcement (or rather deliberate non-enforcement) of bankruptcy provisions is delaying the inevitable. Not only is the inevitable shake-up, and regeneration, of industry and commerce been delayed, the problem (by ignoring both cause and symptom) is also being allowed to build up to the extent that the result of the recession to come will be more severe and damaging than is necessary. It seems that the decision has been taken: feast now, famine later!

Complacency on the rise
The lack of business failure, and the fact that unemployment is still too low, mean that arrogance and complacency is on the rise. Too much good news given too early is not necessarily a good thing. Consequently, unrealistic expectations still abound. Arrogance combined with naïveté (or ignorance) can be a dangerous thing. This mind-set is evident in the inflated property (asking) prices, wage increases (and demands), and negotiating styles (take it or leave it). At the moment, too few Czech realise that they are becoming increasingly uncompetitive, especially when compared with the Asian "sweatshop" economies of China, India, Thailand and Indonesia. The ability of these countries to deliver quality products demonstrate that the Czechs do not have a monopoly in "golden hands". By comparison, Czech "golden hands" also cost a lot more.

Furthermore, few in the Czech Republic appreciate the crucial link between quality, productivity and security (that is, survival). Ludicrous though it may sound, I know of at least one dinosaurish Czech company which, though already patently uncompetitive in both quality and price (and is insolvent), has seen fit to raise both prices and wages! Talk about rewarding poor behaviour and punishing the customer!

Yet not all is gloom and doom. Happily, one cannot help but notice that as the realities of the market economy are finally filtering through, there are emerging signs that, increasingly, vendors are awakening to hard facts:

- Competition is growing – both in their traditional and targeted markets;
- Foreigners are not necessarily people with more cents than sense;
- There is a definite relationship between demand and supply;
- It is necessary to create a favourable and impacting first impression (thus, marketing, service standard and corporate imaging are important); and
- That the customer is increasingly the party who will dictate the terms (the sooner firms learn the golden rule – *he who has the gold makes the rules* – the better it will be for the country as a whole).

Another integral part of the present Czech culture seems to be the baffling perception that contracts may be set aside with impunity. There also seems to be the belief that the time to begin negotiating is after the agreement has been signed. Sadly, I have come across one or two local lawyers (though they are probably the regrettable exceptions) who do not seem to understand what professional integrity is all about, or that they are being paid, not so much to define the law, as to solve problems. For this reason, I am delighted that commercially oriented and professional international law firms are now making their mark on the development of this country. Regrettably, the laws are still unclear and often confusing, and the legal system is still under-resourced. As one cannot yet fully rely on the legal system to provide peace of mind, it is vital to ensure that the deal-path is really clear before implementation.

Secondary insolvency

Investors should also beware of the crippling disease that is plaguing many a company – secondary insolvency. Secondary insolvency exists where a company becomes insolvent because its customers are insolvent. A well-managed company I know recently received a substantial order from a reputable West European importer. The order was firm and the customer was willing to provide a guarantee that payment would be effected immediately upon despatch of goods. However, because the Czech manufacturer was technically insolvent, the bank refused to cover the working capital required for the order. Not surprisingly, the sale was lost.

Privatisation
A company's lack of liquidity is frequently exacerbated by its new shareholders. Most companies privatised through coupon (or voucher) privatisation are controlled by Czech institutional investors (investment funds). Many of these funds are unwilling or unable to put up development capital, or to provide the management assistance, for the cash-strapped companies in their portfolios. Consequently, some of these companies will not make it. CEOs spend too much time trying to resolve their cash requirements by having numerous meetings with banks, creditors, debtors, and, of course, their board of directors. Because of perpetual fire-fighting, such companies lose direction – and truly important matters are left untended. This is a crying shame as a decent proportion of the companies in this bind are basically sound. They deserve support as they have the ability to compete – given adequate resources and time.

It is therefore surprising that when approached by investors offering development capital, some Czech funds will actually refuse to consider offers that involve the devaluation of existing shares below the price (the funds) entered at. The fact that there may be no other lifeline for the company appears to be of little concern. Neither is, it would appear, the prospect of future capital gain (for the funds). Recently, a fund representative cautioned me not to even think for a moment that they would consider giving our investor-clients a majority stake in a company we were discussing. The company was in dire financial straits. Yet the fund representative could not fathom the notion that 5 per cent of a profitable company (as the company could become) could possibly be worth more than 20 per cent of a failed one. In negotiations, it is always worth spending the time to build bridges and to educate the other party to focus on issues rather than positions.

The reasoning for the "dog in the manger" behaviour of beleaguered fund representatives is shockingly simple: if we were to do any deal that effectively realises losses on shares in our portfolios we would have to recognise these losses on our accounts. This would make us look bad, and our investors would go elsewhere (and we would lose our jobs). Much better to allow the companies we hold shares in to continue operating even though they might be increasingly losing the capacity to survive. Our banks will not pull the plug on the companies (as yet).

The fact that some funds are owned by banks does not help the situation at all. It should be obvious that this is where there could be a potential conflict of interest.

Competence
Having discussed motivation, let us address the exacerbating factor of competence. All too often fund managers have little knowledge of how to appraise companies based on fundamentals and the soundness of business strategies. Likewise, representatives of funds who sit on the Boards of companies are frequently poorly trained and ill-equipped. As such, they are unable to add value to the companies they are meant to help. These men and women cannot always be held responsible, for I have come across typists who have been promoted overnight to fund managers, without receiving the basic grooming or induction required.

Several CEOs I have spoken to have complained that, to justify their presence, fund representatives have cultivated a penchant for blocking any change that they do not fully understand. Through excessive conservatism from above, opportunities to survive are being stolen from privatised businesses.

Perhaps even more damaging to the Czech Republic is the toleration of financial corruption, which gives rise to dire conflicts of interest.

Yet in the Czech Republic, conflict of interest is widespread and seemingly accepted, as it probably also is elsewhere in Eastern Europe. Many believe that the malpractices will end with the conclusion of the privatisation process – for the opportunities will disappear, so they argue. This is naïve. Corruption is an attitude which, when housed in a creative mind-set, will find new and more sophisticated manifestations.

Legal processes
When added as an ingredient to the ever present legalistic and bureaucratic processes (these can be lethal!) that remain as legacies from the days of the "old structure", corruption will continue to delay, frustrate and reward that which should not be condoned. Until this aberration is controlled, it will continue to constrain the true potential and development of what is otherwise a beautiful and magnificent country.

Moving further into the microsphere, inexperience and lack of management and language skills in companies, constitute another major area of weakness which needs to be taken into account when considering any investment proposal. Marketing, sales and financial management are the three biggest, and most evident, weak links in the majority of Czech companies. The inability to communicate and report effectively is another serious problem area which may cause rifts internally, as well as with investors. Bringing in Czech-speaking expatriates as interim managers and coaches should be seriously considered in most major-stake investments. Systematic and progressive training is likely to prove essential if the investment is going to fulfill expectations.

While there are other problems that might blight investors, those mentioned above are the main ones that any foreign investor needs to be culturally prepared for. Local in depth knowledge and patience are prerequisites to successful investment action.

Despite the problems in getting things done in the Czech Republic, it is a country with a golden destiny (regardless of what recent capital market performance may suggest). Together with the Slovak Republic, it stands out as the safest bet in the former Comecon bloc. Like Singapore, Korea, Taiwan, Hong Kong and Japan, the Czech Republic has not been blessed with natural resources. It is, however, similar to the "dragons", been blessed in terms of location and with a tradition of industrial ability. In the not too distant future, the Czech Republic may yet return as a leader in the production of world-class, value-added products.

Consolidation
Even at the present time, Czech (as should Slovak, and other Central European) manufacturers must take the initiative to join hands within industry groupings to penetrate new growth and high-yield markets – especially the booming Asia-Pacific markets. Therein lie the greatest threats – as well as the most enormous opportunities. With the passage of time, the threats will grow and the opportunities may well diminish (as they are exploited by others, for example, the Poles and Hungarians).

Through consolidating and presenting together as a united Czech force with others in the domestic industry (even competitors), individual enterprises will be able to market more with more of an impact and effectively. At the same time, they stand a much better chance of achieving superior cost-efficiency and productivity.

The lesson that the Czechs should learn from Japan and other "dragons" is that fierce domestic competition is healthy, but the world is the main prize – a big prize enough, for the time being, for the entire Czech industry to share. The true "enemy" is from without rather than within.

The concept of industrial clustering can be applied at all levels and in novel ways that will maximise, for those involved, the cost-return equation. The same principles can also be deployed regionally (intra-regional clusters). The development and siting of enterprise zones, together with business parks and industrial complexes with good infrastructures may achieve, within a relatively short period of time, what traditional *laissez-faire* development models may never achieve. Time is a luxury the Czechs do not have. *Carpe diem!*

It is unfortunate that Asian investors are still too preoccupied with the likes of China, India and Vietnam, to be truly enamoured of the Czech Republic – or any other Eastern European country for that matter! Still, many of the macro- and micro-economic development models used in Asia, especially in the development of the new little "dragons" (Thailand, Indonesia and Malaysia) are highly relevant for the development of the Czech Republic.

Avoid the pitfalls
As central authority in relation to regional matters becomes increasingly devolved to local authorities, the opportunity for radical synergy through co-operation between the latter and local businesses will be nothing short of phenomenal. I look forward to seeing the realisation of these concepts I have long espoused, in regions of high need such as Liberec, Jablonec and Ostrava.

It is refreshing to note the swell of interest in Eastern Europe, and in particular in the Czech Republic, over the last year. By the time this article appears, the ground swell should have developed into a full flood. Problems relating to the vital investment issues of custody, securitisation, and proxy should, hopefully, have been resolved by this time.

There is, however, the daunting prospect that not all Western institutional funds will be able to fully invest the funds raised. To avoid this problem, investing institutions need to get their own houses in order. It is unrealistic to expect a newly appointed fund manager (regardless of the pedigree of his MBA) to handle investments throughout Eastern Europe – as well as Turkey and Greece, to boot! The only way investment managers can do a good job, is to have the quality ground support that can only come from having good "local guides". Such guides should not only be a good source of relevant knowledge (or preferably, prior knowledge), but they should also realise the importance of clear and timely communication. It is also highly advantageous for the guides to be well connected.

A word of advice to would-be foreign direct investors in the Czech Republic: avoid the pitfalls that have blighted numerous mergers and acquisitions in Britain over the years. The majority have failed to achieve their strategic aims. The reasons? Broadly speaking, failure resulted from:

- Unrealistic expectations (especially concerning speed of realisation, returns and costs); and
- Cultural incompatibility.

I would suggest, especially in the Czech Republic, that cultural differences will be the main cause of failure. If the experience of the British has been so disappointing, how much more so will the results be, when the attempt is to meld different cultures and languages!

Yet, let nothing I have written put you off investing. Volumes have been written on the attractions and wonders of the Czech Republic. I should know, as I have contributed to the existing plethora of the "why you will love living and investing in the Czech Republic" material. However, nobody should ever enter a new market wearing a vision-inhibiting pair of rose-tinted glasses. Ergo, this article to balance the picture.

Finally, I conclude thus, that preparation, research and planning and above all (subscribing to the urgent exhortation of Sun Tzu), "the effective use of local guides" are imperative activities. To cut corners or skimp on these areas would be nothing less than indulging in false economies.

Article by Dr S.L. Quek
First published in "Global Management 1996"
Sterling Publications Ltd.